OVER THE FALLS

A Mother's Story of Navigating
Addiction & the Teenage Years

Elizabeth Anthony

WESTBOW
PRESS®
A DIVISION OF THOMAS NELSON
& ZONDERVAN

This book is a nonfiction work as told according to the best recollection, perspectives and beliefs of the author. Names have been changed in some cases to protect certain individuals and relationships. Errors in circumstances or facts are purely unintentional.

CScripture quotations are taken from *The Message: The Bible in Contemporary Language* by Eugene Peterson, NavPress, Copyright © 2002.

WestBow Press books may be ordered through booksellers or by contacting:

WestBow Press
A Division of Thomas Nelson & Zondervan
1663 Liberty Drive
Bloomington, IN 47403
www.westbowpress.com
1 (866) 928-1240

ISBN: 978-1-5127-6550-2 (sc)
ISBN: 978-1-5127-6551-9 (hc)
ISBN: 978-1-5127-6549-6 (e)

Library of Congress Control Number: 2016919433

Print information available on the last page.

WestBow Press rev. date: 1/13/2017

CONTENTS

THOUGHTS FROM THE AUTHOR vii

ACKNOWLEDGMENTS ix

FOREWORD xiii

1 GROWING UP 1

2 ENTERING THE RAPIDS 15

3 OVER THE FALLS 20

4 NAVIGATING ROUGH WATERS 32

5 THE PEOPLE 40

6 A BROTHER 46

7 FAMILY 51

8 MY TASK 53

9 THE MOVE 58

10 A LEAP OF FAITH 67

11 MUSIC: A SOURCE OF HOPE 71

12 FEAR 78

13 BOUNDARIES 80

14 OUR CALLING 85

15 GRIEF 89

16 FOR EVERYTHING A SEASON 94

17 ANSWERED PRAYERS 98

18 PAIN THAT HEALS 102

19 THE END IS NOT THE END 107

THOUGHTS FROM THE AUTHOR

If you had told me a few years ago that I would be writing this particular book, I would have been horrified & scared to death. Someone did come to me and suggest that I write a book, and shared the story they felt I needed to share. That Facebook message in November of 2011 was a seed that was planted. The events that would transpire in the next two years (almost to the day) are so clearly visible now, it's as though there was a paved path laid out before us that we just had to follow. My story is one of profound sadness and loss through addiction, and of the beautiful redemption that is possible through a real pursuit of faith in Jesus Christ.

I'm not talking about being religious or saying or doing the right things in order to look holy – that's not my story. I'm talking about a living, breathing, active and daily faith without which, I and my family may not have survived. My story is about a journey to a total surrender to self; laying down daily what I want and doing what I feel God is asking of me. My journey has been about, IS about, learning to turn my first born daughter completely over to Him. It was, and is, about learning to trust that there was light when all I could see was darkness.

Mike and I have had to make some incredibly difficult decisions and choices regarding our daughter. These choices were not at all popular with our family and some of our friends. Some people distanced themselves from us and many "believers" questioned our actions. All I can say is that I truly believe that we acted out in obedience for what God wanted for us and for our family during this time.

Truth be told, it would have been WAY easier to go with my feelings and enable Kaci and allow her to manipulate me in order to have the feeling that she was safe, or that we still actually had a relationship. I don't claim to have it all figured out. I am no expert. I struggle almost daily with the lessons I have learned, am STILL learning, and with what God asks from me. I have learned to live my life one day at a time and be present in each moment. I have no demands or expectations for tomorrow.

I don't care about prestige or fame or money. Telling this story is something that the Lord has laid on my heart; therefore, it's His, and He can do whatever He wants with it. My prayer is that just one parent who is going through the same thing will read this and have hope for their future; that they will read this book and feel like they are not alone, and not judge themselves so harshly. Parents who have never gone through a child going off the rails cannot relate or understand why something happens and this, more often than not, leads to casting judgement. We always want a straight answer and a logical explanation of the "why", but most times there is no explanation.

This book has brought immense healing to me. I pray it does for you as well.

Elizabeth Anthony

ACKNOWLEDGMENTS

*Be Obedient. Even when you do not know
where your obedience may lead you.*

- Sinclair Ferguson

This book has been an act of obedience, but it would not have happened without the obedience that many people exhibited by speaking into my life. We always have a choice. We have free will. We can choose how to respond to our feelings, environment and those promptings in our spirit. I have talked about wanting to write a book for over 15 years. I started one and just didn't "feel" it. This book was not what I initially had in mind, but that is the beauty of living a Christ centered life. His plans and His ways are always better than mine. Many times it is hard to see how the current set of circumstances could be better than what I thought I wanted but that is where trust and faith comes in.

To my husband Mike: Without a rock solid partner to share life with, I dare not imagine my fate. I was truly given a gift in my husband Mike. I don't know if he fully understood what he was signing up for when he proposed to a single mom of a beautiful little girl back in 2000. His steadfastness and strength in all of this has been a godsend. There have been so many times that our life together should have been ripped apart. I know there were times that I was less than stellar to be around. Thank you, Mike, for sticking by me and showing our kids true commitment.

To my daughter Kaci: Thank you for chilling me out, growing me and teaching me how to love unconditionally. You've made me a better person.

To my son Brody: Your care and compassion for others has renewed my strength so many times and blessed me immensely.

To my parents, Tim & Sheila: Our road together has been bumpy. Thank you for sticking it out. Here is to us finishing well together. I love you!

To my in laws, Harry & Judy: You have been wonderful encouragers and cheerleaders in so many of my pursuits. Thank you for believing in me!

To my pastor, Paul Vallee: You taught me how to live a disciplined life. You set the stage for my journey with your months of preaching on Job. Thank you.

To Carrie Posednikova: Thank you for reaching out to me about my need to write. It was a seed that has come to fruition. We share some common experiences. You are not alone.

To Brian & Dianalee Walrond: Thank you for speaking into our lives and praying with us. Your gentle ways of encouraging this project forward have been so appreciated. Your spoken word has kept me going and "What a difference a year really makes!"

To Adeline Blumer: Thank you for being real and sharing your journey with me. You have emulated obedience even when it has been completely illogical and terrifying. I have been so blessed to have you in my life. Thank you for your financial contribution to making this book happen.

To Mike & Lori Bourgeois: Your hospitality in the middle of our crisis was such a blessing. We are an oddly matched friendship but share a history and faith that will forever bless me just at the thought of you. Keep doing what you do!!

To Bikers for Christ Mountainview: You were there when it all went down. You **prayed** with us, cried with us and were Christ to us in our darkest days. You dropped everything to help.

To Venture Academy, Gord & Teresa Hay: We were led straight to you. Your obedience to do what you do every day has changed our lives forever. Our family functions completely differently now because of you. Your willingness to help and support us cannot be put to words. We love you guys so much.

Terrie & Bruce Ellwood: Thank you for being a mom and dad to Kaci when we could not. You were chosen for so many reasons to love on Kaci. Your gentle strength was a shining light to Kaci and we are so grateful for your influence in our lives.

And finally, my editor Danielle Klooster: You took a raw manuscript and turned it into a beautiful work. This book would not nearly be the piece it is today without your gentle insight, suggestion and dirty digging. You challenged me to go further with my writing and your suggestions have been so welcomed and appreciated. I look forward to working with you on our next project. Blessings and so much love to you!

FOREWORD

Oftentimes, the painful honesty of others, particularly in Canadian culture, is uncomfortable. It doesn't take us long into adulthood to realize that our society values strength and success, and shuns weakness. In an effort to feel good about ourselves and worthy of societal acceptance, we put on a bright face, hide our problems and suffer in silence. Even in the church community, this culture has largely been adopted. In many cases, we have taken this false culture to new heights, making strength and success signs of spiritual greatness. Problems are often viewed as a consequence of sin in our lives, a punishment of some kind, or at the very least, a lack of faith. Honesty and vulnerability about troubles and problems might cause people to withdraw from relationship, or even pass judgement (this is usually an attempt to make ourselves feel better and safe, because "This can never happen to me. He/she is having this problem because [insert judgement here]").

So, maybe over the course of reading Beth's story, you might feel uncomfortable, maybe even angry. You might wish that she had sugar-coated things a bit, or you might be tempted to pass judgement. You might disagree with some of her decisions. Instead of allowing yourself to get caught up in those "weeds", try this: sit in those feelings. Ask the Holy Spirit to reveal to you the root cause of your feelings, and when He does, submit those things to Him. There's healing for you there. This book is more than just a mother's story; it's an opportunity for each of us to learn to be honest, to learn to love others more fully, and to learn the true meaning of strength and courage.

Discovering the roots of your own grief and pain, and receiving healing, is just one of the treasures to be found in this book. The truth is that when someone chooses to make themselves vulnerable, to open up and talk about the things in their lives that are less than perfect, it creates a safe environment for all of us to "get real". The truth is that, in writing this book, Beth is showing leadership. She is modelling for us how to be humble and authentic. And believe you me, this is no easy task. She risks misunderstanding, judgement, and even rejection from family, friends, and the body of Christ. I encourage you to elevate your thinking above trying to decide whether this mother did the right or wrong thing at any given moment, and to instead focus on the courage it takes to tell this story, and the example set for all of us, to get honest about our stuff, and to live out our faith in an exposed, genuine way. This is the real gift to you that is offered in this book.

Having said all of that, I do want to say something about boundaries, which I think might be the most challenging issue for many in reading this book. I think most of us fail to understand the critical importance of setting healthy boundaries. Often, if we were honest, we'd have to admit that we are often more concerned with how we are being perceived ("I don't want my kids to hate me"; "People will think I don't care about my kids"; "What kind of Mom would I be if I wasn't 'there' for my kids?"), than with what is actually best for everyone in the situation. Organizations like Al Anon, for example, teach family members how to set good boundaries, and not become sick along with their loved one. The research supporting this approach is abundant. The fact is: if you allow yourself to become caught up in enabling and facilitating the addiction, you become part of the addiction; you are a contributor to its continuance. This is a hard truth. As tough as it is, parents have to come to the place where they recognize that having the entire family compromise its commitment to health, safety, security and freedom is no gift to the child experiencing addiction. In the end, the addict needs their family to be free and healthy to that when they are ready to be free and healthy themselves, "family" is a safe place.

Mike and Beth, Brody and Kaci are all showing us, in this story, not weakness and failure, but rather, amazing strength, sizeable courage and unwavering devotion to one another. They are committed to finding ways, through incredible challenges, to support each other and grow together. These people have pluck. Their story is far from over, and they know, as Beth says in the final chapter, that while it's silly to expect a "happily ever after", God always gives us opportunities to find peace and joy whether we're resting in still waters, riding the rapids or going "Over the Falls".

Danielle Klooster

Editor

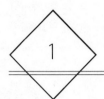

GROWING UP

I was born and raised in Alberta. During those years, I remember thinking how lame it was that I was an average white kid growing up in Alberta, Canada. I would dream about what it would be like to live in Ontario or something; funny how we see things. I was raised in a Christian home with a stay-at-home mom, and a dad who worked in forestry. We moved a lot. By the time I graduated high school, I had lived in eight communities and ten different houses. I remember wanting, with each move, to just have some place I could settle in and call home; a *forever* home. When people would ask me where I was from, I froze… I didn't have an answer. I remember thinking to myself that I would never put my kids through the heartache of repeated moves.

My teenage years were rough. There was a lot of legalism in our home and very little relationship. I rebelled and made poor choices. Even though these choices were bad for me, I still made them, because I could. I was not close with my parents or siblings, even though we lived under the same roof.

When I was fifteen, I went to a family camp at Alberta Beach, to a church camp I had been going to every year, and it was there, by the main gates, that I met Mike Anthony. Who knew, at fifteen, that I would be meeting my future husband? He said he knew, from the minute he met me, that he wanted to marry me. What guy at fifteen has marriage on the brain? We've been raised to believe that most of the time they have other things on their minds besides marriage, but Mike was thinking about a future with me.

I moved out twice during high school, and the day I graduated, I left and moved to Canmore, Alberta. "Finally," I thought, "my life is mine to live". That summer was great. I worked two jobs in order to have some money for spending. During the day, I worked at the Best Western Green Gables Inn as a house keeper and in the evening I worked at Wendy's. The end of the summer came and all of my coworkers/housemates left for college or university, and I was left living alone in staff housing.

Around the same time, I was able to transition onto the front desk, but doing the Night Audit, a midnight to 8AM shift, five nights a week. After several months of this not only was I feeling incredibly lonely, but I also felt stuck. I wondered what I was going to do with my life. I had no idea how to apply for college, or even where to start looking, and I felt that there was no direction from my parents.

Loneliness does funny things to people. By the spring, I was desperate to leave the area, or do something - anything! Little did I know that a weekend in Calgary with an old girlfriend would change everything. It was there that I met my future daughter Kaci's biological father. Rob (not his real name) was cute and super charming. By the end of the weekend, I had no idea what I was getting into, but I was head-over-heels. On one hand, life became super exciting, and on the other, highly stressful. Within

2

three weeks of meeting Rob, I was pregnant. I was panicked, and though felt the impulse to come up with a story for my parents that sounded better than the truth, I did end up telling them the situation.

Mom and dad were pretty adamant that we should get married. I had no relationship with them at this point, but I still, on some level, really wanted their approval, so I agreed. I married Rob after knowing him less than two months. The next four months were a nightmare. We moved – the one thing I hated most in life - three times in that short time period, and I never knew what the day would bring, nor even whether or not we would have food. Without my knowledge, he took out credit in my name, and when I finally left 4 months later, I discovered that he'd racked up $10,000 worth of debt. So I was alone, pregnant, without a job or any way to pay this debt, or even live.

With my tail between my legs, I went home to my parents and waited out my pregnancy. I felt so ashamed and unloved, and was so traumatized by the previous six months that any time anyone would raise their voice I would recoil and start crying. I had been stuck in an abusive relationship, and it had not been not my first. It had taken its toll. A few weeks after arriving home, I called my friend Mike to apologize for something that had occurred between us, some not-so-nice circumstances for which I was responsible. I felt so undeserving, but he forgave me instantly. Our friendship was rekindled. Over the fall of that year, I went and saw a bankruptcy trustee and a lawyer and started the process of getting divorced and filing for bankruptcy. I often cried on Mike's shoulder. I told him everything that had gone on in those tumultuous six months. He was always there. We fell into a routine of talking every night at 7PM; these conversations were my lifeline.

Kaci Abigail was born at the end of January, one month shy of my twentieth birthday. I wanted her from the moment I knew she was "meant to be". Not planned by me, but very much planned by God. He knew exactly what I needed at that time. I needed a purpose, a reason to clean up my life and get on a better road. Kaci did that for me. I had her dedicated – a tradition in some Christian denomination that replaces child baptism where the parent(s) commit to raising the child in the ways of the Lord - on Valentine's Day. I stood at the front of the church as a young single mother. Mike attended, always supportive, but we had no idea what we were in our relationship at that point.

SIDE BAR

Baby Dedication is a funny thing. I see it so differently now. The whole point of baby dedication is to acknowledge that our children are a gift from God. That ceremony is where we give them back to God. We say that we are trusting God with their life. Have you ever really thought about that? As you prayed these big things for your child's life have you ever really considered the road that will be required to get there? When you ask that God would raise them up to be mighty warriors for him, do you just assume that is what's going to happen?

It's kind of like wanting to be all buff and strong and asking God to make you that way without ever setting foot in the gym. Muscles actually have to be torn to grow strong. Ever work out your legs then try to walk the next day or use the bathroom? It hurts! It's safe to assume that being a strong Christian is going to take us, and our kids, through some major pain.

Be careful what you ask for; you may just get it!

After our Mommy-daughter six week post-delivery check-up, Mike came to my parents and picked me up, as I had decided to move to Fort McMurray. As we headed north, I remember feeling terrified that I was going to be raising Kaci alone, but happy that Mike was my support system - my only support system! Mike had arranged for me to rent a room from a lady at his church, so Kaci and I would have a home of sorts. We were there for about five months. After a misunderstanding between me and the landlady, Kaci and I found ourselves desperately in need of a new place to live.

And then, right on time, we met Trooper (Don) & Kathy Minard. Mike had been hanging around with a few bikers from the church, and we followed them on a ride one sunny Saturday in August. After a great day and lunch at the diner in Marianna Lakes, Don and Kathy asked if Kaci and I would like to come and live with them. Don and Kathy had two little boys, Robert and Joshua. As she was a stay-at-home mom, Kathy offered to babysit Kaci so I could go to work. I really wanted to get my own place, and so I only ended up staying with them for a month or so, but it was such a blessing. Kathy insisted on approving the suitability of the apartment I was being offered through low income housing, and after receiving her blessing, I moved into my first real home with Kaci.

Over the next few years, Mike and I got married and moved briefly to Sparwood, BC. It was there that we had Brody. Shortly after Brody was born, Mike was able to adopt Kaci. We told her that she and daddy were going to get married. Mike's family surprised us at the adoption ceremony, and bought Kaci a beautiful navy blue silk dress in which she could twirl, as well as a little ring to her, from Daddy. It was a great day, and a great time in our lives. God brought a lot of healing during that time. However, a few months later the coal industry, in which Mike was working, tanked, and back we went to Fort McMurray.

SIDE BAR

Education was something that my family always held in high esteem. I felt that there was an expectation that everyone go to university. My dad had a degree, and had been working on his masters while I was in high school. Nobody ever sat down with me and asked me what I wanted to do, nor did they offer any assistance in researching, which was a more arduous process in the pre-internet days, post-secondary options. I always felt like I was not good enough for my parents, in many ways, but my lack of post-secondary education really intensified that feeling. I felt that since I did not have a degree, I was not entitled to an opinion. These feelings of inadequacy - combined with the shame I felt over my mistakes - became a strong internal voice. I really wanted to do everything possible to prove to my parents and the world that I was indeed "good enough". I started by volunteering at a crisis pregnancy centre called *Birthright*. From there, I started volunteering on the local youth justice committee. I was selected for an eight-month community leadership program called *Leadership Wood Buffalo*. At the same time, I attended various community engagement sessions and fundraisers. I was doing all of this while I was working full time, opening a coffeehouse and youth centre called "The Dugout". I would be gone sometimes 4 or 5 nights a week when Mike was off. I was trying so hard to prove I had value that I sacrificed time with my kids. Don't get me wrong; these were worthy pursuits, and even though I didn't know it and my motives were fairly messed up, I was fulfilling part of who I am. The problem, besides the imbalance in my family life, was that I was really desperately looking to others to tell me I was important and valuable. I have a lot of regret over that now. I wish things had been different. I wish I hadn't felt like I wasn't good enough. I wish someone had spoken into my life and just said those words to me: "You are enough. You are loved, just the way you are." I wish I would have read and believed what God says about me and not what others say or think about me, or what I thought of myself based on my perceived failures and shortcomings. These feelings of not being good enough would follow me for a long time.

We never viewed ourselves as a "blended family"; Mike was Daddy and Brody was not Kaci's half-brother, he was her brother. We would often forget that Kaci was not biologically Mike's daughter. When Kaci was born, I had given Rob an ultimatum. I told him that he had to choose what he wanted. There would be no coming back into our lives when Kaci was two or five or ten years old and suddenly expecting to be "dad". Either he was in her life or he wasn't; he chose the latter and left us alone.

From the time Kaci was born, I determined that every decision made would be through the lens of "will this help or hurt Kaci?" I did not go out one time without Kaci in her first year of life. I also felt that, in spite of the horrible ending with Rob, that children deserve all the love in the world that any healthy adult is willing to give them. With this in mind, I chose to maintain a relationship with Rob's mother. We never explained to Kaci or Brody how it was that Grandma Val was their grandma and they didn't ask. I was always so appreciative that Grandma Val treated Kaci and Brody the same.

I knew that the day would come where I would have to tell Kaci about Rob. As she was growing, I had a lot of fear that she would be just like him. I did everything in my power to raise her to be kind, honest, respectful, loving and find a faith in Christ at an early age. I would silently beg God "Please don't let her become like her father".

Kaci was a wonderful little girl. She was so cute, and as she got older, she began to discover her gifts. She was - and still is - a free spirit. She loved to be creative. She danced, sang and loved to draw. She loved to bake and would decorate any surface she could with abstract design. It used to drive me crazy. When she was six, I felt like it was time to tell her that our family was unique. I prayed for wisdom on how best to do this and God showed me.

Kaci grew up in a two-parent family. The concept of a blended family was not even in her realm of understanding. So I decided the best way to go about this was to introduce the idea through a bedtime story. The first time I told her the story, she did not like it, and was almost crying. She said: "Mommy that is not a very nice story!" Just like that, I knew she was not ready. Over the course of the next eight months I would gently re-tell her the story of her life (changing names of course), and the last time I told her the story I asked her: "What do you think of the daddy that went away?"

So matter of fact, she replied, "Mom… He just wasn't ready."

It was then that I knew she herself was ready to hear the truth.

I never told her that Mike was not her dad. That would have been a completely false statement. Mike **was** her dad. In every sense of the word, Mike was her dad. I explained that God has a plan for everyone's life. And God, in his wisdom, knew that the man it would take to create her (because God planned her from the beginning) was not going to be the man that would be her daddy. It was then I reminded her about her and daddy getting "married" and that was when he adopted her.

Over the next five years or so, Kaci would occasionally ask questions about Rob and I would always answer them. Sometimes we would call Grandma Val and she would answer Kaci's questions. The summer after Kaci turned thirteen, she was reading some books her Nan, Mike's mom, had given her, in which they were discussing blended families and children. Kaci came to me and asked if she had any other siblings. My heart dropped. I had never lied to her about Rob, but I only ever gave her enough information to satisfy her. I didn't want her to know she had three sisters, because I knew she would want to meet them. That would mean opening the door to Rob and the past, and I was completely overwhelmed at the thought. But I knew it had to be done; I couldn't lie and it was her life, not mine. We called Grandma Val and she talk to Kaci about Rob's other children.

By this time, we had moved to Red Deer. Moving to Red Deer from Fort McMurray in 2008 was a dream come true. We made this move as a lifestyle choice; Mike was still working in Fort McMurray, and commuting in and out for his six-day rotation. We had bought our "forever" home in a wonderful neighborhood and were settling into our new life, a much slower paced life than the one we had lived in Fort McMurray. No volunteering or fundraisers or working full time for me! The city itself was a lot slower paced than Fort McMurray and I was working just part time in a very non stressful job. That fall, I invited close to 30 people for Thanksgiving dinner. But, just hours before everyone was to arrive, my elbow and right arm started to ache and go numb. By the time we finished cooking dinner, I was unable to use my arm. By the next morning, my left arm and both my legs started tingling and going numb. I started to feel scared, and asked Mike to take me to the walk-in clinic because I felt like something was really wrong. While waiting to see my doctor, the left side of my face started to go numb. The doctor, upon hearing my description of the symptoms, instructed Mike to take me immediately to the emergency department at the hospital. Then I got really scared! A CT scan of my head was done, but nothing abnormal was found. The doctor said he didn't know what was wrong, but informed us that they were referring me to the Multiple Sclerosis (MS) clinic to start the process of possible diagnosis. Aside from times I had been afraid during domestic violence situations, I could not recall a time that I had been so deeply frightened. We were not a family with health issues. Aside from my grandmothers having high blood pressure, nobody in my family had even been sick before. No cancer, diabetes, heart attacks – nothing! This was a whole new experience, and we had no frame of reference.

The week prior, I had visited, through my job, a woman that had MS. Her disease had progressed to the point where she was in a wheel chair and required assistance in cleaning her house, bathing and getting to the bathroom. My heart broke for her. I thought about what it must be like for her, being alone, navigating a disease that had no rhyme or reason in its symptoms and trying, day after day, to live as normally as possible. Little did I know what I would face just one week later.

MS is a funny disease. It's not something that can be diagnosed in a week or even a month; it's something that can take up to a year. Needing a year to diagnose an illness that leaves you unable to work is less than ideal. Day after day, my condition worsened. This first episode lasted roughly six weeks. I was exhausted all the time. The intense pain I felt everyday was unbearable. I could only find relief sitting in the hot tub. The strongest pain meds did nothing except make me stoned. I could still walk to the bathroom, but just getting there and back was enough to need a nap. I couldn't raise my hands above my head to even wash my hair. Mike had to do that for me.

Mike's work schedule meant he would be gone for six days and then back home for six days. The kids were only six and eight at this time and my condition, along with their dad's absence, put them under a lot of stress, which, in turn, made me feel extra stressed. I could see fear in their eyes about what was happening, but there was nothing I could say to change it. I felt helpless, like I was failing my kids.

At one point, Mike took a full cycle off of work to stay home with me, but of course he did have to go back. As a result, helping with homework or hanging out with the kids had to happen in my room. There were a few times where Kaci would have to make Kraft dinner for Brody for supper because I had no energy to get out bed. I remember feeling that I was so exhausted that even my muscles holding my bones in place were growing tired, as if all my bones could fall to the back of me while lying down then it would help me not feel so tired. After about six weeks, the pain subsided and I was able to do a little bit more. I was still exhausted and unable to work. I had gone for my first MRI as part of the MS diagnosis, but would have to wait another six months for the next. I learned very quickly that our healthcare system is not designed to get people well as soon as possible. I felt like I was left to rot at home. For years we had paid into critical illness insurance in the hope that if Mike or I ever got sick that it would be there for us. After actually getting sick, I learned that the only way that they do pay-out is to have a diagnosis. With my diagnosis still months away, we were very disappointed that we had paid into the insurance for nothing, or so it felt. This led to a lot more stress and burden.

I don't remember at what point I made the decision, but eventually I decided to go seek help outside of the traditional mainstream healthcare system. I had never entertained the idea of a naturopath doctor, but I was so desperate I thought: "Really, what do I have to lose at this point?" I made an appointment at with a doctor that my mother in law had been seeing. After several appointments, and way too many dollars, I realized that he was actually a kook who did nothing to help my condition. After that we took to calling him Dr. Kook. Finding humour helped ease the disappointment a bit, but not much!

One Saturday morning in April, I was talking with Grandma Val, who told me about another naturopath in Medicine Hat who rented space in her daughter's store. I called and booked an appointment, and we made our travel plans to head down to Medicine Hat. This doctor was completely different. He spent close to an hour and a half asking me all sorts of questions. He was the first doctor to ask me about what my stress levels had been prior to getting sick.

Many of the questions did not seem at all relevant, in my mind, but I answered them anyway. At the end of the appointment, he was able to tell me with absolute certainty exactly what was wrong: in addition to a low functioning thyroid, I had a severe case of adrenal fatigue. The long and short of it is that the ten stressful years I lived leading up to our move to Red Deer had taken its toll on my body. When I moved to Red Deer, for the first time in my adult life I had three months of rest. It was needed, but my body crashed and burned. All the buildup of stress caught up with me. I was prescribed various supplements and vitamins and each bottle's purpose was thoroughly explained. I was told how I would know when my body was healed and which symptoms would leave last. He was clear that I needed to make some serious life adjustments in diet, exercise, and stress management, in addition to following the treatment plan.

Because the treatment would actually heal the damage that had been done to my body, not just mask symptoms, he was clear that while I may start feeling better within a month or two, I may not see complete reversal for year. I left there with some hope and started my treatment immediately. By the fall of that year, I was able to go back to work on a part time basis. I was grateful to have a second chance at life. God showed me a lot through that time of illness. I learned that life was too short to spend my time desperately trying to be accepted. He healed that pain in me, along with the feelings of not being good enough. I stopped feeling the need to do things in order to feel accepted. I learned to take care of myself and most of all I learned to say "no." Not only that, but I learned to say it without giving a reason or excuse. My motivation for doing things changed; it was actually very freeing. I had nothing to prove anymore. I could just be me. It was then that my Type-A personality shifted and I started calling myself a "Recovered Type-A". I joke about it now. Am I still driven? Sure, but my motivation is so different. I am nowhere near as busy as I was. Mike and I agreed that I needed him as my compass moving forward. I now don't commit to anything long term without chatting with him first. He can always see when I am taking on too much.

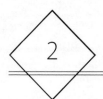

ENTERING THE RAPIDS

A couple of years into our time in Red Deer, I was working in a short-term contract at the United Way. My contract was ending in December, and I had some anxiety about finding another job to start in the New Year. Looking for a job at the end of a budget year is not a good situation in which to find oneself.

My personal faith, at this time, had all but fizzled out, and church was something we did because the kids wanted to go, but was not a top priority. Growing and becoming more Christ-like was a thought and a yearning, but my bible would be left unopened for months at a time.

It kind of seems like, throughout my life, there were periods of time when a major life decision or change presented itself, and we could see how God directed it; then there would be long periods of time in which we would disengage and lose focus and it seemed like God would let us be. He was always waiting for us, never pushing, but looking back, I see His hand in it all.

While at the United Way, I got a call from the church we were attending. We had been attending Living Stones Church roughly eight months or so and I volunteered in the coffee bar. But this call was not from the coffee bar coordinator; it was from the senior pastors' executive assistant, Kimberly.

I remember standing in my co-worker's office at United Way, confused as to why Kimberly would be calling. After a minute or so on the phone exchanging pleasantries, I was able to put together that they wanted me to come in for an interview.

Now, it's important to say that, while I had been applying all over the place trying to secure a job, I had not applied at the church. In fact, I had no idea that they were hiring. At the time it wasn't even an option for me, really. I wasn't one of **those** people. You know the ones: they look like they have it all together and are uber spiritual, bible school-educated people. I was just an average mom who had been working in non-profit for six years and trying to raise a family. Truth be told, I had struggled for years with the structure of church and wasn't a huge fan of the whole idea. God, yes. Jesus? I struggled with that but had worked through it. But the rigid rules and structure of church? I wasn't a fan.

I agreed to the interview. I suggested that maybe I should bring my resume with me, even though, to that point, they had not asked for one. In fact, they had given me the impression that perhaps the job was already mine, and this interview may be just a formality. I was taken aback by the entire process, but also intrigued.

The next day I met with the senior pastor, Paul Vallee, and his executive assistant, Kimberly. He glanced at my resume, but was more interested in talking about my strengths, and detailing for me what the job would entail. There was to be a board meeting that week and he said that it was pretty much a sure thing, but would call on Friday to let me know one way or another.

Between that Tuesday and Friday, I had two other organizations call me for interviews. I went ahead and booked them, since nothing was set in stone. Mike and I had sat down and talked about my job situation and the pros and cons of each position. He too had some hesitations about the position at the church. It was the least favourable as far as pay was concerned. Over the years, Mike and I had both struggled with the business/administration side of churches, and to go work at one felt like we may be crossing over to the "dark side".

I hadn't prayed about a job position in years but figured that if I was going to work at a church, maybe I should, so I prayed about it. It's funny to think about it now that we're out the other side. Over the next three days, I felt only a resounding sense of peace about taking the job. I knew it was not by chance. I thought about the Facebook message a friend had sent about writing a book, and then this potential job offer had come, and it was all very clear to me that I needed to get in the proverbial car and trust, because God was taking me on a journey.. This was happening. I just needed to agree and do it.

Two weeks later, I started at the church and it was weird. I had either worked in business/non-profit settings my whole life, places in which the work environments were such that you kept personal stuff personal and things were always professional. On my second day, we had a chapel time and staff meeting, which I discovered was a weekly occurrence. Co-workers prayed together. They prayed for each other, and for everyone in the church, and I realized in that moment that being there was so much bigger than me showing up to a job every day, that somehow the work we were doing had an eternal impact. The weight of that was overwhelming, but I felt so supported and safe in the process that it felt doable and right.

I had entered a spiritual greenhouse. This was a time to be nurtured, cultivated, and pruned, to thrive and grow in a safe place. I met every week with Pastor Paul for mentorship. He modelled discipline in all areas of his life and challenged me to do the same. He taught me the importance and necessity of discipline in how I spent my time both at work and at home. He didn't just sit there and tell me how I should live; he **showed** me every day. I started putting God first and taking the time to read and meditate on the word and pray daily. I started journaling my thoughts and prayers and reflecting on them. I started taking better care of my physical body. This was an especially big deal as I was 50 lbs overweight and very much an emotional eater.

Prior to this season, I had lived my life as most people do, making decisions and living based on how I felt. For example, I had tried to lose weight many times before, and had always failed. That is what happens when you try to do things in your own strength. Change is hard; it doesn't just happen. I learned that overeating is viewed the same in scripture as over-indulging in alcohol. In Christian circles, or at least in the ones that I grew up around, drinking was a big no-no, but nobody ever said anything about stuffing yourself until you were sick, or even having seconds at supper. Somehow that was always okay.

I had to surrender this part of my life to God. I prayed that he would take away the desire for the unhealthy things and change me. I prayed for self-control and had to daily commit myself to submitting to God's perfect will for my life. I started using a popular phone app to help plan my meals and teach me about proper portion sizes. I also joined an all-ladies' boot camp style class. I knew I needed to lose weight, and I had a short timeframe to get in shape. On the September long weekend, my whole family was planning to gather in the Crowsnest Pass to celebrate my grandfather's eightieth birthday. My dad's side of the family is quite active and love to do outdoor activities together. As we were all going to be together anyway, we planned to climb Crowsnest Mountain. I knew I would not make it even half way if I didn't lose some weight and strengthen my muscles.

In four months, I lost 20 pounds and gained all kinds of muscle and energy. There were many hurdles along the way - no pain no gain, as they say - but on the September long weekend I climbed the Crowsnest Mountain. Although I did not make it all the way to the top, due to extreme wind that made it feel too unsafe to continue the last 20 minutes or so, I made it ¾ of the way to the top - all the hardest parts! I pushed through the mental obstacles and got to share some great moments with my family. I was very proud of my accomplishment.

3

OVER THE FALLS

That fall, Pastor Paul started a sermon series on the book of Job. Now for anyone who has ever read the book of Job, it's not exactly the prosperity, love, grace and feel-good lesson on which most people choose to focus. Most believers like to lean more toward scriptures like Jeremiah 29:11, not to Job, who, let's face it, is kind of a buzz kill. It was during these sermons that I felt totally deceived. I had heard many prosperity messages over the course of my life and I do not ever remember hearing the part that we will **share in Christ's suffering.** This was a major revelation. I felt like I had bought and paid for the goods only to find out that the warranty completely stunk. I wanted my money back! This was **not** what I had signed up for when I committed my life to Christ… to suffer? I wanted blessing, joy, peace, happiness - anything but suffering. Like, really, who really, truly, knowingly signs up to suffer? No thanks!

Over the next few weeks, Pastor Paul helped me work through my thoughts and feelings. He prayed with me and encouraged me that the journey was worth it.

It was during this series in Job that we started to see and witness some disturbing behavior in our daughter Kaci. She started saying that she wanted to be able to do whatever she wanted. She said didn't need school. There was a defiance in her that was never there before. She had turned thirteen that year, and up to that point had been a real joy to raise. She had always done well in school. She was - and still is - a very talented artist, like my sister Caroline, and loved to create, dance and sing.

Mothers have so many hopes and dreams for their children. College, travel, careers, family - we truly want all of the good things that life has to offer. When troubles come, those things can suddenly start to feel like they're slipping out of reach. It's hard to know how to deal with the fear, frustration, and disappointment. In November, we got a call from Kaci's school that she had gotten into trouble during lunch. They asked if I could come to the school to meet. I had a brief conversation with Kaci on the phone, and for the first time ever she didn't sound like my kid. It was like she was someone else. She began to tell me that she didn't want to live with us anymore. I left work, a total basket case, and bawled all the way to the school. What was happening to our family? I was baffled! What in the world had happened to our daughter?

Mike had been commuting to Fort McMurray for close to four years and was away at work for his six days "on", so I had to go deal with this alone. I was escorted into a board room where a school counsellor and Kaci were sitting. I looked over at her and for the first time in my life I felt like didn't know her. Gone was my hip, fun, artsy girl and she had been replaced with a very angry, defiant looking teen. In the course of a couple of months, everything about her seemed to have changed - her likes, her dislikes, style of clothing, attitude, sleep patterns, food intake… everything.

My journal entry from November 6th of that year read:

"Lord I need a miracle for Kaci. She is in a dangerous place and feels she has learned everything she needs to know in life. HELP!! The potential is there for her to self-destruct, and I want your very best for her life. Father, only you can change her heart. Lord, help me to guide her. Help me to give up control to have influence. Open Mike's eyes to that fact as well. I am so scared to lose her. Show me how to minister to her or bring another adult into her life that can speak into her life and guide her...AMEN~~

As we met, Kaci was defiant, rude, nasty and completely unreasonable. Half way through the conversation she apparently had enough of listening to us, stood up, walked out and was gone. Frantically, I called Mike, and he started the seven hour trip home back to Red Deer.

===

SIDE BAR

Prior to this, I, as many good Christian parents do, believed that a child was a reflection of their parents and things like this didn't happen to good parents. *"**Obviously**,"* I arrogantly thought, *"it only happens to those who are not good parents."* This, by the way, is a load of rubbish! Many times I judged those with teenagers who went off the rails, thinking: *"Obviously you didn't spend time with your kids like I spend with mine. I'm an engaged parent who talks with and spends time with my kids."* Oh, the arrogance I had in thinking that my parenting was somehow so superior to others!

I will say, without arrogance, that I really believe I was a good mom. I was – am - a good mom. People came to me for advice and guidance. My problem was that I allowed myself to become puffed up. I really thought I had everything figured out…then my bottom fell out.

In the weeks leading up to this, Kaci had told me that she thought she had learned all she needed to in life and wanted to drop out of school. She also made comments implying that, should anything happen at home, she already had a place to stay lined up, at her friend's house. When Kaci officially went missing during that meeting at the school, I remembered those comments, went home and started making calls to all of her friends that we knew.

After a call or two I was able to locate her, though I couldn't get her to agree to return home. In the span of the next five hours, she phoned home five times. It was very apparent that she was dealing with a significant internal struggle; on one hand, she wanted to rebel, and on the other hand, still very much loved her family (and would say so on the phone every time she called).

SIDEBAR

We instilled in our kids from a very young age that we would never go to bed or leave the house angry at someone. Life is short, and nobody should ever live with the guilt that comes from someone's last words being anything but loving.

By seven or eight pm we were able to convince Kaci to come home. She came home and wouldn't say a word, but stayed with us, watching TV and eventually falling asleep in our bed, where she stayed until Mike got home around 3AM from Fort McMurray. She later told us that she had felt bad, and that was her way of trying to smooth things over. It seemed a little odd to be watching TV together after such an intense day, but I think we were all trying to make things normal again.

The next morning, we kept both of the kids home from school to be together and have a family meeting. As I was seeking the Lord that morning, I prayed for wisdom regarding how to deal with everything. After that prayer, I came up with the idea to create a two-part survey for the kids, asking questions about our family, about us as parents and what their idea of the perfect way for a family to function.

Part one was to understand if we had communicated the rules and expectations for our home well.

1.   What are our expectations of you?

2.   What are the rules in our house?

3.   Why do you think we have these rules?

4.   What happens when the rules & expectations are not followed or kept?

5.   What should our goal as parents be in trying to raise you?

Part two was to solicit feedback from the kids so we could better understand where they were at in their thinking and attitudes.

These questions and their answers would give some structure to the conversation we would have later.

1. What does a healthy family look like to you?

2. What areas do you feel we do well at parenting?

3. What areas do you feel we do badly at parenting?

4. What freedoms or privileges do you feel you deserve as kids?

5. What are you willing to do in order to get those freedoms?

We used the answers from the survey in our discussion. Kaci's and Brody's answers were very different. This exercise was quite valuable in helping us understand. Kaci had asked if she could go and spend a few days with her aunt, and we agreed, so on Wednesday, Mike took her up to Edmonton and dropped her off. On Sunday, we went back to Edmonton to pick her up. I was hurting so badly, feeling like a failure, and so let down, that I felt like Kaci was the last person I wanted to see at this point. Normally, I am a pretty up beat and bubbly person, but on the drive up, I never spoke.

Kaci was home just a few days when she lied to Mike. He called her on it. Around 9PM I heard screaming coming from outside. The door opened and I stood there watching a very emotionally charged screaming match on the front porch. As the argument escalated, Brody, who also had come to see what was happening, became visibly distraught. Finally, I called our close friend Chris, who is an RCMP officer and asked her to come over and try to talk to Kaci.

She took Kaci down to her room, closed the door and stayed there with her for what seemed like an eternity. Kaci was adamant that she was not spending the night at our place, and not at Chris's either. Chris agreed to drive her to a friend's house. Brody didn't want to be there, either, and who could blame him? The last place Mike and I wanted to be was in that house that night. We all felt like running away. We called Brody's youth pastor and Mike took him over to spend the night at his house.

It was a sleepless night. The next morning, Mike and I sat in the living room looking at each other helplessly, not knowing what to do. While still processing the night's events, we could not bring ourselves to notify any family. But we did have a group of people, however, who were not blood related, but played a very significant role in all of this: the Mountainview Chapter of ***Bikers for Christ (BFC).***

BACKTRACK / REWIND

A few years before all of this happened, I had been praying for Mike to find some good, godly men to have as friends. One day, he said that he was going to go for a ride on his bike, and would be gone a few hours. He headed down the highway and stopped in to the A&W in Innisfail, a town just south of Red Deer, for a coffee. He parked his bike, and found that in the parking lot were a bunch of bikers from the Mountainview Chapter of ***Bikers for Christ***. He was intrigued. After that, Mike started hanging around with them and spending time at the chapter elder's farm, east of Bowden, another small town along the QEII corridor. They had a shop full of bikes, parts and lots of dogs, all of which Mike loved. He bonded with Bud and Deb immediately. The group was pretty small at this time, with only four patched members and their wives.

Over the course of the next two years or so, the group grew to nine members plus wives. It was that group that dropped everything and arrived at my house during our crisis, the afternoon after the big porch fight.

My living room was full of our biker family. They prayed with us and, just by their presence, made us feel like we were not alone. At times I did feel overwhelmed with everyone there, so I would just go and sleep for a while. Everyone was totally comfortable and accepting of whatever we needed. Mike, in particular, was very much sustained by their presence.

All of the **BFC** had either gone through this themselves or had children who had gone through rough times. Just knowing that we had a shared experience, to me, made these people experts on the topic. The experts were not the counselors or parents with **perfect** children. Everyone always has advice, but that doesn't mean they have a clue what to do in our particular situation. This group understood and respected that truth.

I really believed that Kaci would come home that day, or at least call, but she didn't. At supper time, we decided to call the RCMP and report her missing. I reached out to one of her youth leaders, Kodi, and asked him to pray. Within an hour, he texted me back and said that the Holy Spirit told him where she was, and that he was going to get her.

We learned through the guidance counsellor at Kaci's school that Kaci had been dating a kid who was a known drug dealer and that she had been hanging out with a tough crew. In no time, Kodi called us back and told us he had found her. Off he went to the Collicutt Centre (a large rec centre a few blocks from our house.) When Kaci spotted him, she bolted. He chased her into a bathroom, where she barricaded herself in a stall. He relayed all of this to us, and stressed that we needed to get over there immediately.

SIDEBAR

Kodi later told me that not only did the Holy Spirit show him where to find her, he also provided protection. When Kodi walked in and through the Collicutt to find her, there were close to 100 people that he knew there. He had all the backup he could ever need.

Mike and I, along with multiple bikers, drove over to the Collicutt where Kaci was now being held in a stair well by a security guard. It is my understanding that the security guard intervened during the bathroom scene, and they walked together to the stairwell. We immediately called 911 and requested assistance.

When I saw her I was shocked. She looked nothing like my Kaci. She was high, and white as a ghost and clearly agitated. She started to give me attitude until she noticed Deb and Connie, two of the *BFC* wives, were right behind me. Her expression quickly changed to that of "Uh oh!" and man, did Deb ever give it to her. Kaci just looked like a scared little girl.

Two female RCMP officers arrived and asked to speak to her privately. After twenty minutes, they came to talk to Mike and me. Because she did not, in those twenty minutes, express that she wanted to harm herself or others, they could not legally take her to the hospital. A feeling of total helplessness came over me. I asked what we could do. We were told that in order to have her hospitalized and assessed, we would need to get a court order.

The decision was made that Kaci would go out to Bud and Deb's farm for the night. There was no way she could run from there. After the police searched her, she was placed in the back seat of Deb's Ford Ranger, and with Marissa, another of our friends who was also a *BFC* wife, in the passenger seat, they headed south to the farm. Bud took all of the knives and shoes and locked them in his shop and checked on her every hour throughout the night. Looking back, I am so grateful and amazed at how the *BFC* crew was there for us through all of this ugly stuff.

Emotionally drained and totally exhausted, Mike and I went to bed. It was not at all a restful sleep. We woke up at 6AM and were standing outside of the courthouse before 8AM.

As you can imagine, I had shed enough tears to fill a swimming pool by this time. Little did I know that this was just the beginning. I felt helpless and out of control. As it turned out, going before the judge was such a God thing. We prayed for favor, and I prayed that I would be able to hold it together enough to communicate our concerns. We were the last on the docket for the day. This was done on purpose, to give us privacy, and aside from a social worker in the room, it was only us, the judge and the court reporter.

The judge asked me why we were there and I read off a list all the behaviors and things we had noticed and were concerned about, and explained why we needed this help for our daughter. By the grace of God, I was able to hold it together and the order was granted. The judge shook my hand and told Mike and I that we were wonderful parents, and thanked us for caring enough for our daughter to do something about it instead of writing her off or putting the responsibility on Child Services, as happens in so many cases. It was a comfort to have this reassurance.

After the order was granted, a warrant for Kaci's arrest was issued. That was the crappiest feeling I had ever had, and not the highlight of my life as a mother. Arrangements were made with Bud and Deb to bring Kaci into Red Deer to meet us at the police station where Kaci was transferred into a police car. As she was cooperative, they did not hand cuff her. She would not even look in our direction. We drove behind the police car to the hospital. All I could think was "Wake up… this is just a bad dream." It was a bad dream all right - a living nightmare!

Kaci was placed in a hospital room and guarded by a police officer, where she stayed for four hours until she could be seen by a doctor and then the child psychiatrist. Without that court order, they would have released her, saying "She's a thirteen year old girl who is rebelling", but, because of the court order, she was admitted to Unit 39 – The child psychiatric ward. We were called when she was admitted, and told we could come and see her in the morning. So, we went to bed, once again emotionally drained and completely exhausted. It was in Unit 39 that Kaci got a first-hand lesson in what things are privileges, like having her own clothes, and what things are rights, like hospital-issued pajamas and food. The freedom she so craved was completely taken away.

A couple of weeks prior, I had been reading in my devotions and a scripture stood out to me. It's not a popular verse that everyone knows. Psalm 127:2. The last part of the verse says: "For he grants sleep to those he loves." That scripture has stayed with me since, and through the turmoil of the last several years, and to this day, I speak and declare that scripture over my life, and have not had any major issues sleeping. During this initial difficult time, sleep was such a gift. I was able to sleep soundly and wake up feeling rested and ready to start my day. These days were full of turmoil but they would somehow always end with resolution so we could sleep. I was so grateful for that.

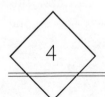

4

NAVIGATING ROUGH WATERS

Over the next five days, we went to see Kaci daily. The nurses told us that we were excellent parents that clearly cared about our child - though I sure didn't feel like an excellent parent at that point! Most of the kids there wouldn't see their parents even once during their stay. When we were not at the hospital, we were racking our brains to come up with a plan. We knew had to do **something** - but what? I wanted Kaci out of Red Deer and away from the older kids and the Collicutt. I wanted her off drugs. I wanted her safe. I wanted all the anger to go away. I wanted her to find peace again. I wanted her to want to finish school.

We had no idea what was out there in terms of help or treatment. I sat down at the computer and started to Google: Teen Addictions…Treatment Centers…Military Schools… Boarding Schools…

We know people who had gone through the **Teen Challenge** program, which is a Christian residential alcohol and drug rehabilitation centre; however, in Canada, one has to be eighteen, so that was a no-go. I had very little success in my search, except for this one site that kept coming up on the computer screen. It was **Venture Academy,** and it looked like it might be an answer to our prayers. Their website claimed that they were Canada's leading program for troubled teens. They were not just a rehab centre, something we weren't completely sure we needed at that point, but they also specialized in teenagers experiencing any number of issues including negative peer pressure, school suspensions, low self-esteem, and drug and alcohol abuse. Additionally, they offered help for things as far ranging as mental disorders, depression, anxiety and everything in between.

Mike and I sat down at the computer and listened to the testimonials and we both agreed that this was exactly what we needed. I feel I need to stress here that making the decision to send Kaci away somewhere was not about us not wanting to deal with her. She needed real help, and seeing the school counsellor once a week was not going to cut it. This was so much bigger, and Kaci needed a "pause" from life to get to the root of why she was struggling, and to find a place to begin healing. I had to admit to myself that, although I could choose what I felt was best, that I could not give her what she needed in this time in her life, and had to look to a "village" to help me with raising my child.

I liked that the **Venture** program was based in a community and not a "wilderness experience". I had seen some "boot camp" type experiences like that for troubled youth, but was turned off because, at some point, a person has to go back to the real world and reintegrate. To me, it would not be beneficial to isolate someone from the outside world. In saying that, though, the program does prohibit all social media at the school and in the homes as well as phone calls to anyone who is not on an approved list. All calls are scheduled.

33

Though I felt very strongly about this decision, as I wanted to do everything I could for her, I never wanted her to feel like we had given up on her or that our love was conditional. I did not want to respond to her the way I had been responded to when I went through my struggles in my teenage years. I responded the way I wished my parents had responded to me. Through my own shortcomings early on as a parent, I learned that when you choose to become a parent, you take on the highest calling that God has for your life. There is no position, role, business or volunteer opportunity that is as important as raising your kids. As believers, we will answer for everything we do – and don't do - in raising our kids.

Real love doesn't always look like hugs and kisses and presents. Sometimes real love is **not** doing those things, because it enables bad behavior. Although it goes completely against natural parental instincts, sometimes it is very necessary. What it all boiled down to for me was that I needed to know in my heart of hearts that if anything ever happened to Kaci and I had to bury my daughter, I could look myself in the mirror and have no regrets about what I had done or not done to try to help her - even if that meant bankrupting ourselves.

I called the 1-800 number listed on the website, and a man answered the phone and identified himself as Chris. Instantly, I felt very comfortable. Chris was very understanding and empathetic about our situation. I remember having a feeling of confidence in his ability to know what needed to happen. After the call, I filled out and submitted the very long online application, and the next day we got a call back that Kaci was a good candidate for the program. Then there was the conversation about cost… this was all new to me and I had no idea what 24/7 care looked like. I was taken aback. How on earth were we going to pay for this program? I felt so strongly that we were being led to **Venture,** but I had a hard time wrapping my head around the cost of private treatment. The upside was that there was no six-to-twelve month waiting list, like there are with most publicly-funded programs – maybe it's just me, but when people are in crisis, it seems a little outrageous to expect them to wait a year for treatment!

The people at **Venture** told us we could come immediately.

Sometimes we have doubts over whether or not what we are doing is the right thing. I had felt so strongly about the decision, but once it was made, I had my moments of uncertainty. I was very sure that this was what God wanted for us, but, just in case I needed a confirmation about whether Kaci needed to be at **Venture** or not, God gave it one morning before we went to see Kaci at the hospital. I had reached out to my friend Justin, who ran an organization for children in foster care, and had asked what resources they might have for us. He didn't have anything specific, but did ask me to come by, because he had a book he wanted to give me that would help me to better understand what was going on with Kaci and what we could do to help.

When Justin handed me the book, I started to cry, right there in his office. The book was called: "Hold on to your Kids", by Dr. Gordon Neufeld. Dr. Neufeld has done extensive research on the idea of attachments and wrote the theory on attachment. As it turns out, the entire **Venture Academy** program is based on his methodology. I thanked Justin, ran down the stairs and got in the car. I turned to Mike and said, "If you need confirmation on **Venture**, here it is!" I handed him the book, and we looked at each other and absolutely knew this was what we needed to do.

When faced with a situation like this, it is easy to let pride get in the way of asking for help. We had always been the ones to help others, and having to reach out to friends and family was very much a humbling experience. Some family members felt we should keep this to ourselves. I don't know if that was because it was embarrassing for them or what. But I had no desire to pretend my life was ok when, clearly, it was not.

We met with extended family, and some agreed to help. Another family member paid for our flights, and a close friend gave us the money for the initial registration fee. It just sort of came together.

We had some friends from many years back who had just relocated to Kelowna that past fall. Although we were Facebook friends, and I would send them one of our annual Christmas letters, we had not spoken in several years. Once again, I put my pride aside, reached out to Mike and Lori, and in one paragraph asked if they might have a couch available for us. Lori told me later that she thought my Facebook had been hacked! She asked me to call her. I did, and she was more than happy to give us a place to sleep. Little did I know the significant role Mike and Lori would come to play in this journey. Let me tell you: this couple is the real deal.

For whatever reason, I felt like I needed to reach out to our friends and family and tell them what was happening. I know this is completely opposite of what most would do. My perception was that there is a lot of shame attached to a situation like ours and many believers feel that, just because Christ is in their life, it means that they need to look perfect even when things are falling apart; that somehow if there is an admission that life stinks that it means that God's promises of blessing and prosperity cannot be counted on. I reached out and emailed all those people in our lives that meant something - both believers and non-believers – and, without sharing every detail, told them that life was not okay, and we were in a place of desperation. Prayers were welcomed! Here was what I wrote:

Dear Friends and Family,

I am writing to you because you mean something to us in some way, large or small. We are in the middle of a family crisis and I apologize for the impersonal email.

We are having some big challenges with Kaci. Over the last several months, our daughter has turned into someone we don't know.

Two weeks ago she ran away for the first time. We were able to convince her to come home, but a week later, she ran away again and did not return to our home. We had to go to drastic lengths to locate her, and proceeded to obtain a court order to get her admitted into the hospital for assessment. She has been in the youth psychiatric unit at the Red Deer Regional Hospital since Friday. We have since learned she does not have a mental illness and her challenges are behavioural (this is a good thing!).

We have made the difficult decision to send her to a behavioural treatment program in Kelowna BC for a minimum of 30 days, for assessment, treatment and intense counselling. After many days of research, we believe this is the best option for Kaci to have a chance to want a future for herself and learn to love herself again. She needs to get away from the negative friends she has surrounded herself with and take some time to focus on herself and learn some tools and life skills to assist her in becoming a successful adult. When she returns home, we will be starting home schooling with her. Family counselling will be a part of our lives for many months to come.

If you are interested in checking out the program the website is www.ventureacademy.ca

Please keep us in your prayers as we go through this difficult time. We will be leaving tomorrow to take Kaci to Kelowna and will be working to put our lives back together while she is away. This has really thrown us for a loop and are looking forward to being able to live as a family again.

Thank you for being a part of our lives,

Beth & Mike Anthony

Sharing the plan with Kaci was ugly. We went to the hospital and told her, and she started to cry, and became very angry. We again saw the internal conflict, in that, on one hand, she was rebelling and wanting to live like an independent adult, and, on the other, she was still very much attached to her parents. Because of Kaci's emotional state, the nurses suggested that we should leave. When we got up to go, Kaci grabbed me and wouldn't let go. She clung to me as thought her very life depended on it. She was screaming "Mommy, don't leave me… please…I'll be good I promise… I don't want to go to Kelowna - Please!!"

Nothing that had happened up to that point ripped open my mother's heart like that moment. Mike and I left the hospital, both in tears, and when we got to the car, I collapsed over the console into Mike's arms and I cried harder than I ever have in my entire life.

SIDEBAR

I often hear from people that they feel bad when they hear that someone is struggling and they had no idea. Here's a little secret I've learned: *life is messy.* It's hard, too - for everyone! All people go through stuff that is hard: divorce, cancer, broken relationships, loneliness, finances... whatever. We do a pretty good job of hiding it because we think that to be vulnerable is to appear weak. In fact, the opposite is true: vulnerability actually shows strength. It cuts through the junk and faces life for real; the raw, painful, sometimes messy, mascara-running-down-your-face-with-snot-dripping-down-your-nose kind of real. Everyone has pain and it is how you deal with it that determines the outcome.

5

THE PEOPLE

Before going to see Kaci on the day we shared the plan with her, we had made plans to meet up with any **BFC** members who might be available later that day, at the Starlight Diner in Bowden. After the hospital ordeal, being in a restaurant, looking and feeling like a hot mess was not a very appealing thought to me - to say the least - but I knew Mike needed to see them before we left for Kelowna.

Dinner was pretty low key. Kaci called and apologized for getting upset and told us that she had now accepted the fact that she was going to *Venture* and was willing to go. This was a big step, and a huge relief! After dinner we went outside and huddled in a circle in the parking lot. Everyone took turns praying for us. It was a nice send-off. I recall feeling loved and glad that we took the time to allow the **BFC** to love on us.

We went home and packed for our trip. The hospital had only agreed to discharge her early because we had a plan in place. We would pick Kaci up the next morning, and then head straight to Calgary to get on a plane for Kelowna.

I wasn't able to book the flights until we had confirmation of Kaci's discharge and, as it worked out, we had a couple of hours to kill in Calgary. In those couple of hours, we took Kaci to see a friend of Mike's. Kaci really looked up to David Brunning. He was, and still is, a graffiti artist and biker. Kaci had met him on a motorcycle ride with Mike and they really hit it off, both being artistic, and graffiti was something to which Kaci was really drawn.

We hung out at David's apartment and he shared with Kaci a little bit about what he had learned throughout his own rocky life. They talked about art, and Kaci soaked it in like a sponge.

During the entire time leading up to Kaci's admission, I was super stressed, worried that she was going to bolt. Although she had accepted the fact that she was willing to go, I knew she didn't want to, and I feared she might change her mind at any moment.

Arriving in Kelowna, we took a cab to our hotel and went for supper. What do you talk about at dinner after the ordeal of the last few weeks? I was pulling at straws. We sat in silence mostly and, after supper, walked over to Walmart to grab a few things that had been on the **Venture** required list of items.

The next morning, Mike and Lori, the couple allowing us to bunk in, showed up at the hotel with their minivan so we would not have to cab around with our luggage. After not seeing us for so long, I was amazed at their willingness to jump in and help. The fact that they loaned us their van for the day and re arranged their family's schedule for us blew me away. I was grateful just to have a place to sleep! I didn't expect anything else. I mean, it's not like we were close friends or family. Our history dated back almost eight years, but we hadn't spoken in a long time until this situation arose. Another blessing in the storm!

We arrived at the school house and met with the intake staff. We were given about twenty minutes with Kaci and a counsellor, so our goodbye was quick. This is done intentionally by **Venture**, to minimize dramatic and emotional departures. Kaci was taken offsite for her intake and orientation, and we were left to meet with one of the owners and head of admissions, Teresa Hay. We were given a questionnaire of two hundred multiple choice questions about Kaci's behaviors and reactions to things. There were questions about our family dynamics and everything in between. They dove into every area you could imagine. Teresa had a way about her: a strong confidence, a calming demeanor that said she knew they could help. I so appreciated their desire not only to help Kaci, but that they took our specific family morals/values and beliefs into consideration.

This program is not Christian, but it is holistic in its approach. They acknowledge that health, nutrition, exercise, creativity, hobbies, and spirituality are all parts of a person. But because it is so highly specialized and each child has their own customized treatment plan, they work to incorporate all of these areas into helping a child get well. When Teresa was made aware that we were Christians, she opened up and shared that she and her husband were as well. We found out that Kaci had been placed in a host family home with a couple that were not only highly skilled professionals but were also believers. Bruce ran a local gymnastics club and Terri was a parent consultant and educator specializing in Gordon Neufeld's Attachment Theory. My heart soared and I knew in that moment that God was very much directing our path, and my little girl was exactly where she was supposed to be.

Intake took almost 4 hours, and by the end of it Mike and I were both completely exhausted. This day had been so difficult.

Aside from Kaci going on a holiday once or twice with her grandparents, she had never been away from us for more than a night or two. Now she was going to be gone for who-knows-how-long. Not only that, but we would not be allowed to see or speak to her for the next thirty days. We would, however, be allowed to send letters once a week. The letters were given to her on a set schedule, and she could reply, on a set schedule. That rule was really hard to take, but, at the same time, there was a little part of me that was a bit relieved. I hated to admit it, but I needed a break from her, and from the situation.

We picked up Lori from work in her van and headed back to her house for some supper and R&R.

SIDEBAR

Throughout my whole adult life, I had been an emotional eater. If I was stressed out, I ate. When Kaci first ran away and the "ride on the rapids" began, I couldn't eat. If I did, I would throw up. Earlier in this book, I mentioned that I was always able to sleep even when the days were filled with turmoil – partly because it seemed we could almost always get to a resolution at the end of the day. It was the same with eating at this time. I would not be able to eat all day, but would be able to eat a little bit at supper time. I lost twenty pounds in three weeks this way. Not the healthiest way to lose weight, but I guess it was a little perk.

We stayed in Kelowna for a couple of days afterward to make sure everything was ok with Kaci. Mike and Lori were complete rock stars. They loved on us and Mike toured us around Kelowna like a tour guide. He brought a little bit of normal into a chaotic time. Our 24 hour update call came when we were at the Mission Hill Winery - not the best place to be crying! Luckily, it was during the week, so we were the only ones there, beside staff.

When Mike and Lori moved to Kelowna from Edmonton, they had decided to rent for a while, so they could get to know the community and figure out where they would want to buy. They rented a house on Pritchard Drive. Pritchard Drive is in a highly desirable area of West Kelowna. One side of the street backs onto the lake and the other there is a canal for boats and a tree farm. Their house was a haven. It backed onto the tree farm below the Mission Hill Winery and their back yard looked like something out of a California movie. It had an in-ground kidney-shaped pool with a multi-tiered concrete deck and a hot tub. Although it was fall, it was still beautiful, and was our sanctuary, our place of calm in the storm.

Mike and I felt that we needed to take a couple of days just to breathe and absorb all that had happened, and to just be together. We needed some perspective, and we knew just where to go to get it.

Mike's Uncle Derek and Aunt Lorraine, who lived in Victoria, had successfully raised four kids. We had always wanted to visit them, and now seemed like the perfect time. The other Mike drove us to the airport, and offered unlimited support any time we needed to come to Kelowna. Hugs were exchanged, and we were on our way.

Uncle Derek met us at the airport and had us laughing before we got to the car. He's known to be a real jokester and there was no time like the present to get started.

We spent four days touring around Victoria. It rained most of the time but being December it was sure better than snow. We went to the Butchart Gardens, with their *Twelve Days of Christmas,* and then fed the seals in the bay. I got my first introduction to David's Tea, which I decided I love, and we ate a lot! My appetite had finally returned, which was another blessing. Uncle Derek and Aunt Lorraine had been in our shoes several years earlier with their oldest daughter, and to hear both sides of the story offered hope. I listened intently to their advice and took it to heart. Aunt Lorraine talked about seasons and constantly reminded me that this would not last forever. They do come around. It was hard to imagine.

I was sad to leave Victoria, but knew I couldn't avoid my life forever. We flew home and picked up Brody and went to a house - our house - though it didn't feel like home anymore.

6

A BROTHER

It is very easy to forget, in the middle of a crisis with a child, that the other children in the house are affected as well. They experience their own hurt, and have emotions around the situation. Siblings often feel left out, because the lime light is always on the rebellious child. All your energy, thoughts, prayers and conversations tend to revolve around that child. Uncle Derek and Aunt Lorraine stressed the importance of making sure we continued to date and have sex often, but they also said: "Make sure Brody doesn't get lost in the shuffle".

When we got home, it was the beginning of December. Normally, I would have written a Christmas letter, and we would have had a non-traditional family photo taken, and I would have sent it to 100 of our closest friends and family. We would set up our tree and decorate for Christmas.

Neither Mike nor I had any interest in Christmas. We just wanted it to go away. Learning to do things, based not on how I feel in the moment, but because they are right and necessary, can sometimes be a challenge. We needed some light in our life, so we told Brody he could have as many friends over as he wanted, and we would have a Christmas decorating party. We bought a bunch of appies and snacks, turned on Christmas music and Brody and three or four girls decorated our house for Christmas. He had a good day.

Just before this all happened, we were playing with the idea of homeschooling. I was always somewhat against it, but Brody brought it up almost daily. Brody had always struggled in school. It wasn't because he lacked smarts - he's actually very smart, even brilliant! - But he does not fit the "box" that is school. It's sad that every kid is forced into a system, whether it fits them or not, and then they're taught that their value lies in what they get on a test. I could write a whole book about what needs to change in schools, and I get rather passionate about it so we'll stay away from that for now. The incident with Kaci really took its toll on Brody. He couldn't bear to go to school and answer questions about where Kaci was, or listen to the gossip. He needed some time to just "be".

I was able to negotiate part time hours at work, in order to attempt to homeschool Brody. I say "attempt", because I feel like I failed miserably. Because we were starting half way through the school year, there was no money available to purchase curriculum, so I had to rely on free online tools and try to piece together some sort of a program. What I could see had been missing from traditional school was that kids were no longer required to learn how to hand write, so I felt that signing documents could be an issue in the future. I took the first month and every day we would work on learning how to handwrite - one letter at a time, and then putting them together to form words. I also identified that Brody could not tell time on an analogue clock, so we did that, too.

Mike and I wrote to Kaci every week, and Brody wrote at least once a month. It was hard to find things to write about. Because of the expense of sending Kaci to *Venture*, and the fact that I gone to part time at work, finances became extremely tight. There was little money for entertainment, but sitting around the house in the middle of winter wasn't good either. We got a family pass to the Collicutt Centre, and went there almost every day. Brody played basketball, or we played badminton, and then we swam and sat in the hot tub. I must have walked a hundred miles on the track – it was a great way to just try and stay sane!

We talked with Brody about Kaci and what was going on, but we censored a lot. There would be no benefit to Brody to hear all of the nasty details. Prior to this I had said "no" to things a lot: No to friends to coming over… No to giving the kids rides… No to making them snacks - they could make their own. Regarding the snacks, my ideas around parenting came from a place of wanting to empower my kids to do things for themselves and not be living in my basement until they were thirty. Through our interactions with *Venture* and learning about the attachment theory, I realized that I had done some things that actually hindered them from developing, and knew that I had to change. I started saying "yes" more often. Friends were always welcomed. Rides to places happened much more often, and I learned how important it is to not give up your authority by allowing your children to prepare and cook their own meals & snacks. It *is* important to teach them to cook, which I did, but when I became the provider of the food, the shift that happened in our family dynamics as a result was nothing short of amazing.

One week before Christmas, just as we were getting ready to head out to Kelowna, we got a call that Kaci and another girl had run away from the program. The police had been called, and they were doing everything they could to find her. Brody had a friend over when we received the call, and even though I was upset and Mike was away at work, I chose not to say anything until after the friend left. I felt it was more important, in that moment, to allow Brody to be a kid and have fun with his friend than it was to cause an upset.

Kaci was located later that evening, and after a conversation with the program staff, it was decided that we should cancel our visit. Kaci was very much being ruled by her emotions at that time, and she needed a strong emotional response from us in order to understand the consequences of her actions. I have to admit, I was somewhat relieved that we were not going. I wasn't ready to see her yet. My heart still felt like it was bleeding, and my anxiety would go through the roof whenever I thought about seeing her. When we told Brody, he was relieved as well. He didn't want to see her. In many of our conversations, Brody expressed his feelings about Kaci and what she had done. I felt like I needed to validate his feelings and not try to tell him that his feelings were wrong. He was very bitter. I said to him, "Brody, it's ok to be mad, but at some point you need to forgive. Jesus forgives us and we only hurt ourselves by not forgiving others." While Kaci was gone, we poured as much love, attention, and affection as we could on Brody. Needless to say, when Kaci came home, it was a hard adjustment. Brody loved feeling like an only child, and when Kaci was back with us, he felt lost in the shuffle of chaos again.

SIDE BAR

I did my best to try and make Brody feel supported and loved during this season. There were times I had nothing to give, and instead just sat there, stressed. Brody has this impeccable, God-given ability of being able to walk into a room and instantly sense if something is not right. He would constantly ask me what was wrong. I struggled with being honest, not wanting to stress him out, too. It can be difficult to balance decisions made regarding one child against the impact of those decisions on another child. Brody needed and deserved stability even in the midst of the chaos. I know he has struggled so much with carrying the burden of these circumstances with him. My prayers for him were, and are, so different than the prayers for his sister. Sometimes I didn't know what to pray that would help him.

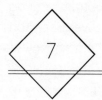

7

FAMILY

I would love to tell you that our immediate families were super supportive during this time, but that isn't entirely true. One side contributed to getting Kaci to **Venture**, but had never dealt with anything like this before, so were at a loss to know what to do. The other had dealt with a similar situation, but didn't have the insight to understand how their decisions in dealing would negatively impact their children for years to come.

I need to stress here that I do not blame anyone for their responses to us, because we realize those responses came from a lack of understanding as to God's leading in our lives and situation. Some advised us to put Kaci in foster care and let her hit her rock bottom - ouch. Other opinions were that **Venture** was just a money grab, and that if they could not "fix" her within three months, it would prove that we were being taken for a ride. I believe that one of those pieces of advice came from a place of wanting to protect us from hurt we were experiencing, and the other from a place of not understanding that counselling and change is a process, and doesn't happen overnight.

Sometimes God calls you to do things and go places that make absolutely no sense to those on the outside - even Christian relatives - and yet, obedience is required. I strongly believe that we were supposed to walk through this valley alone without feeling supported by our families. I read a devotional during this time that I felt confirmed that. The devotion was based on Jeremiah 15:17 NIV, which says: "I never sat in the company of revelers (the crowd), never made merry with them; I sat alone because your hand was on me and you had filled me with indignation (anger)."

The devotional reading went on to describe the verse like this:

"It is certainly unnecessary to say that turning conviction into action requires great sacrifice. It may mean renouncing or separating ourselves from specific people or things, leaving us with a strange sense of deprivation and loneliness. Therefore the person who will ultimately soar like an eagle to the heights of the cloudless day and live in the sunshine of God must be content to live a relatively lonely life. There are no birds that live in as much solitude as eagles, for they never fly in flocks. Rarely can even two eagles be seen together. And a life that is dedicated to God knows divine fellowship, no matter how many human friendships they have forfeited along the way." (NIV Streams in the Desert Bible)

I know our families prayed for us and did what they could. I love them all dearly, and hope that in some way they too can be better through this experience. It is so hard to know the right thing to do during a difficult time, and we needed grace, so I can give grace as well.

8

MY TASK

As the process went along, time began to drag. I often sat at home on the couch, or just lay on my bed, as if in shock, feeling like a zombie. I struggled to get through a day without crying, and it was a struggle not to let myself go into a dark depressing hole. I pulled myself up and went to the Collicutt to walk the track in the evenings, while Brody played in the fieldhouse. I walked and listened to music. On one particular day, as I was walking, I started to pray. It went something like this: "God, this stinks. I walk this track almost every day, all alone. I do everything alone, and I'm getting sick of it. I want someone to walk with me. I need a gym partner!" And that was that; I promptly set the thought aside and forgot the prayer.

When I was done, I went down to the pool for a soak in the hot tub, and something happened to me that had never ever happened before. I was sitting in the hot tub staring into space; I happened to glance beside and there was this petite little thing sitting beside me. She looked like she was about fourteen. We struck up a conversation. She was new to town and asked if I knew of a good place to party. She asked about my tattoos and she let slip that she had got into trouble when she moved to Alberta. I shared with her a story about a friend of ours, and how her parents had sent her to Newfoundland as a teen when she was getting into trouble.

This gal, whose name was Jennifer, said, "Man, I wish my parents had done something like that for me. I couldn't see how what I was doing was hurting me!"

I looked at her and replied, "I'm happy to hear you say that. I just took my daughter to a treatment centre in BC!"

Suddenly, Jennifer blurted out: "I'm a recovering heroin addict!"

Wow! She proceeded to share her whole life story with me, and we clicked instantly. It was a divine appointment if I had ever had one. She had locked herself in her room at her parents' house over Christmas, going cold turkey off of heroin. She was just one month sober that day. We had a wonderful visit, and I felt like I should offer her a ride home.

I introduced her to Brody on the way to the car, and as it turned out, she only lived a block away. Over the course of a week, we saw each other almost daily, and spoke frequently about why she wasn't dead, and how she was coming to believe that maybe there was a plan for her life. I felt like God wanted me to buy her a bible. The idea kind of freaked me out, as I'd never bought a stranger - or someone I hardly knew - a bible before. I found out her favourite color was purple, so I went to the local Christian book store and picked out a purple *Celebrate Recovery* Bible. (*Celebrate Recovery* is a bible-based Twelve-step program).

One afternoon as I was driving Jennifer around to drop off resumes, I gave her the bible. She was quite touched, and carried it with her everywhere. We took her out to meet the **BFC** Crew and she brought it with her there, too. I took her to a couple **Celebrate Recovery** meetings at a local church. After a month or so, she took a job out of town, and we parted company. We still keep in touch from time to time, via Facebook. She was exactly what I needed at that time, and God used that time with her to show me that I had love to give, and that I did know how to love people addicted to drugs, and that I still had value. I realized that although I could not be a mother to Kaci at that time, there were still girls and women out there who needed to be nurtured and loved.

Then there was Tanya. I was introduced to Tanya one Sunday at church. She was new and looking to get connected both with people and through volunteering. As I was in charge of most of the volunteer areas, she was brought to me. She indicated that she was looking for some discipleship and mentoring, and after meeting with her, I felt that she and I would be a good fit together. Tanya was middle-aged, and had just come out of a detox program. She was living at a recovery home for women with addictions. She was just in the process of getting a job, and I delivered a hamper to her house so she would have some food until she got her first paycheque.

Tanya was one of the most beautiful women I'd ever met. She was kind and giving and gentle, in a way. She was not meek by any means, and the years of addiction were apparent in her appearance. She was rail thin, and she looked like she had lived a hard life, but her spirit was gentle. I am grateful that God has given me the ability to see people the way He sees him. I didn't see a drug addicted prostitute; I saw a beautiful child of God.

A couple of months later, when we went to pick up Kaci from Kelowna, it "just so happened" that Tanya needed to be in the area on that exact same day, for a court appearance, to answer for some charges from a year prior. What were the chances of us both needing to be there on the same day? God has a way of setting these things up.

I met up with Tanya on the morning of court. She was looking at potential jail time, and I could tell her nerves were raw. As we walked up the steps to the court house, I stopped and said, "Tanya, can we pray?"

She said, "Yes, please!" and there on the steps of the court house, we gave thanks that God had brought us together in a divine appointment. We acknowledged his power and authority in our lives and his ability to restore what we have broken. We prayed for his will over her life and asked for strength to get through the proceedings.

The judge was impressed with the progress she had made over the previous year, and while he acknowledged that she needed to repay her debt to society, he expressed that he did not want the punishment to derail the progress she had made in her sobriety. He understood the importance of having her young daughter, Kelly, back in her life. Her sentence was house arrest for four months, and then probation. She was allowed to go to work and church, and was court ordered to attend AA meetings weekly. She was required to make arrangements with her parole officer as to when she could run errands and had to keep documentation of these arrangements on her person at all times. It wasn't freedom, but it was much better than prison, and she would still be able to see her daughter - that was the main thing! I was grateful to be able to be with her that day. I also got to meet her elderly parents, John and Natasha. Natasha told me that she was praying for us every day, and also praying for Kaci. I saw them a few times over the course of my time in Tanya's life.

While Tanya was still at the transitional house, I also got to know a couple of the other ladies living there. My life took a drastic turn, and soon I was attending **Celebrate Recovery** almost every week. The leaders of the Newcomers 101 group said if they saw me there again, they would have me lead the class. I never knew how my week was going to look; sometimes I would have to drop what I was doing and go pray with Tanya, or drive someone to **Celebrate Recovery**. This was the job that God gave me to do during this time: I was to minister to women with addictions. This season was a huge time of growing. Even though my life was in chaos and I was living one day at a time, God used that pain to show compassion to and learn from these women. Both Jennifer and Tanya were given to me as examples of what my daughter could be like at twenty-three or forty-five years old had I not been obedient to what God asked me to do for and with her. It was also a promise that my obedience would bring restoration to my own daughter. I clung to that promise.

9

THE MOVE

Mike and I were going out to the farm every week to see Bud and Deb, as we had been doing for a few years. We began to realize that we were getting tired of city life. I had learned to vegetable garden and preserve food, and we wanted some space. We had been looking at acreages, and were looking to the future with concern. We did not want to bring Kaci back to Red Deer, as she would be back to living two blocks from where she had gotten into trouble, and the temptation to gravitate to those same kids was something we wanted to eliminate as a possibility. As the thought took hold in us, the drive to get ready for a move kicked in. I started to pack. We needed to paint the house if we were going to sell it, and it and we needed to de-clutter and de-personalize the house, and decided there was no better time than in the dead of winter.

As our move became public news, I sometimes felt like I was losing my mind. People would ask where we were going. I had no idea. All I knew was that the Lord told me to get ready and pack. I felt as though we were being called to move to the little farming community of Olds Alberta, where *BFC* was based. Being a smaller town, I felt it might just be what we all needed for a fresh start. We got the house all ready to sell and put the sign on the lawn. Because of how little equity we had in the house, and our already tight budget, we could not afford to list it with a realtor. A realtor friend of mine offered to do photos for free, just to help us. Also, as a courtesy, we notified the realtor, Tony, who was the agent when we bought the house. He'd always kept in touch with us, and I wanted to explain the situation and let him know why we were wanting to move.

Tony spent two days running numbers and trying to make it work to list the house. He was willing to forgo his commission to help, and said we would just have to get the money together to pay the buyer's agent. He talked to a lawyer friend of his who offered his services for the transaction for half price. It really felt like doors were opening. The next day we had a call from someone at the church who was interested in looking at the house. I had prayed that a believer would buy our house and use it for the same reasons that God had given the house to us. But that was not in his plan. After viewing the house twice, and getting a signed offer with the condition date approaching, the other party backed out, because of they were worried about a potential future issue with the landscaping. We had never had any issues with it, and the thought that the whole deal would fall apart over something so little was devastating.

The day that the offer fell through, I could feel it coming. I had been in continual prayer all morning, and every time I prayed I got the same answer in my spirit: "This is going to work out, but not the way you think." When we got the call that the deal had fallen through, I was sad but not surprised. It was an emotional blow, but knowing it was coming helped softened it, and I was just left wondering what was next. Often the path the Lord takes us down is full of twists, turns and detours. All these things are opportunities to trust Him and not rely on our own logic.

We had already decided that Brody needed to go back to school, and were confident before this that if God wanted us in Olds, he would sell the house and we would be able to bring Kaci home to a new place. A couple from BFC lived on a farm near there, and had offered their basement for us to live in for a couple months until the house was sold, after which we planned to buy an acreage around Olds. I had enrolled Brody in middle school in Olds and made arrangements for bussing. So when the deal on our house fell through, we wondered what to make of it all. We had already planned to move to the farm that weekend. Mike assumed we were not going anymore, because it didn't make any sense to move to Brendyn and Stacy's place if we had a perfectly good house in Red Deer. I could understand how crazy it sounded when I insisted that we go anyway. Why would we go? There was no logical reason to move to someone's basement, but that's what we did.

We packed our suitcases and brought our bed and TV with us and made the one hour drive to the farm. I was hopeful for our future, and felt like we needed to settle in and start our life in Olds. I had no idea how short lived this would be for us. I had quit my job at the church, and was able to secure some contract employment in Olds. We had been at Brendyn and Stacy's for a month when it was time to go get Kaci; she was being released from the program at *Venture*. Of course, the living arrangements were not an ideal scenario for Kaci to come home to, and to this day I wonder what this was all about. I remember going for a walk and asking God why we were living on the farm - what was the purpose? Life was not great, and we were not at rest there. The answer I felt was: "You are there to serve them." So that is what I did. I helped with the house, and Mike and I both did yard work. If we saw a need, we did our best to meet it. I enjoyed the talks with Stacy and the quiet of the farm.

Exactly six months from the day we had dropped her off, we drove out to Kelowna to pick up Kaci. She had completed her treatment plan, and a graduation ceremony was planned. We stayed with Mike and Lori again; since it was going into summer their yard, and the view, was spectacular.

The ceremony was small. It was only for Kaci, and all of her classmates attended. A couple of them gave speeches; both Kaci and I spoke also. Listening to Kaci's speech brought tears of joy to my eyes and I truly believed I had gotten my daughter back.

Kaci's Speech

I remember the first day I got here. I was so scared. When my parents told me I was coming to a treatment center all I could think of was "Wow, way to go Kaci!" The first day I got here I did not talk. "Yes please. No thank you and sure" were the only responses I could say to anything. Patty was the person that did my intake and all I could think was…."Great, I'm getting help from people who have never had a bad day in their lives" I showed up at Terri's unable to speak, eat or settle in. I started going crazy and I had to call my dad. HE told me everything was going to be ok and I had to do this. I love my family, all of my family for supporting me the way my dad did, writing me every week and listening to me on my calls. I used to think the only good things in life were running away, partying and drugs. Later on I learned that everyone has bad days. Even people who seem perfect.

I've had so many amazing moments with the girls here. Like going snowboarding and totally having to get stitches after a day on the hill. Or going on the bus and seeing a cute guy driving by. I love the girls here for supporting me even when we were not getting along. I admire a lot of you for trying to bury the hatchet with me before I leave so we are on good terms and for supporting me along with my family to the very last day.

I want to thank the staff here as well. Thank you to Reece for being so chill and bringing me poutine after I ran away. That was really good. Thanks to Julia for always being sarcastic to lighten the mood. Thanks to Allen and Bryce for putting up with my insane mood swings and to Leif for bringing us boarding. And to all the other ladies that work here...... for just always putting a smile on my face and always making sure I'm happy and staying on task and motivated.

My mom, dad and family have supported me and prayed for me every day and I am really thankful for that. Thanks to everyone here I am a more reflective, mannered, authentic person and am so grateful for that. Thank you again and I will miss everyone here.

I believed this was the beginning of the end; this nightmare was finally going to be over. Kaci had received intense counselling and support every week at *Venture*, and had dealt with a lot of her past hurts. Though it was a fight to make progress, she had come through it grateful for the experience. Our family dynamics had changed in the process, too. We had learned so much from our weekly sessions at *Venture* and our whole family benefitted. We were filled with hope.

But the transition home was rocky. We had a plan in place, but due to finances, and the fact that it was summer, as well as not having access to support resources in a small town, we struggled to hold things together. We had strict instructions to keep Kaci structured and busy. Too much free time would be a negative for her, we were told. The routine that Kaci had at **Venture** was rigorous, and trying to maintain that level of structure proved to be too much. Kaci was able to get her first real job at Edo Japan, which started out as a good thing. I felt it would occupy her time and give her the means to get her first cell phone. There were some rough days where Kaci's anxiety caused her to bolt from work, and we were sent frantically looking for her. There was more than one call to **Venture** from my car, with me crying, feeling completely helpless.

In addition to our plan to sell our Red Deer house, we also decided to sell the house we still had in Fort McMurray. This would allow us to buy an acreage around Olds and pay off what we owed to **Venture**. However, as soon as we shared this news with our renters in Fort McMurray, they went and bought a place and moved out early. Since there was some work that needed to be done on the house, we took a week at the end of June and went up to Fort McMurray to deal with the house and visit Mike's brother and his family. It was great spending time with them. Dealing with the house, on the other hand, was another issue.

The renters had moved out and cleaned the house but there was a wickedly strong smell when you first entered the house. At first I thought the smell was incense residue, but then I decided it smelt more like cologne or something. I tried everything imaginable to get rid of that smell. I washed every surface of the house with hot bleach water. I left bowls of ammonia around to absorb the smell - nothing worked! When I had worked as a young adult at a hotel, we'd had an ozone machine that would be used to clean and freshen the air in smoking rooms. I figured I would try and rent one, hoping that would fix everything. I called around, but nobody seemed to have one of these machines. I called a company that did clean up and restoration cleaning after fires, floods and crime scenes. They did have a machine but it was going to be $1500 – Ack! That was not going to work. I apologized for wasting their time, and briefly explained the situation. Out of nowhere, the guy said, "Come get the machine. I will show you how to use it. You can have it for $300."

I couldn't believe it! That never happens – especially not in Fort McMurray! I love Fort McMurray, but it seems like everyone is there to get their cut of the action, and everything is ridiculously expensive. God placed compassion in that man's heart that day, and blessed us beyond what we could have hoped.

I picked up the machine and used it according to the directions. 48 hours later I brought it back. It had removed about 80% of the smell, but somehow a remnant still lingered in the air. I was ready to pull out my hair. When I told the company from whom we had rented the machine that it had only worked to about 80%, they were shocked; they used that machine to clean up crime scenes when bodies were not discovered for days. They offered me, free of charge, some fire wash to wash the walls and told me to just bring back whatever I didn't use – another blessing. So off I went again to wash every surface of the house. Twenty-four hours after I finished cleaning the house, I came back and – hallelujah! - the smell was gone. To this day, I still have no idea exactly what that smell was. We left that day and travelled back to Olds, satisfied that the house was in good shape and ready to sell.

We arrived back on the farm to less than ideal conditions. It was a rainy summer in 2013. Calgary and area had experienced major floods, and Olds also had their fair share of rain and crazy storms. People were literally seadoo-ing on the creek, where the water had been no more than two feet high, but was now over six feet high. I couldn't believe it. While we were gone, the basement at the farm, where we were staying, had flooded. Things had already been challenging, as the entire time we'd been staying there, we killed at least ten beetles a day. Upon our return, after the long drive, all I wanted to do was go to bed but when I pulled back the sheets to climb in the bed, there was a beetle – *in* the bed! I completely freaked out. When I managed to collect myself, I looked at Mike and said, "I'm done. I can't stay here anymore. This is more than what I can live with."

We did a full beetle sweep of the bed and apprehensively laid down. We talked in bed about our options. Red Deer? Nope. We knew it wasn't best for Kaci, and the years of having Mike commuting had taken its toll on the family. It only took one more six-day cycle of Mike going to work and me being left with the kids, and I knew I couldn't do it anymore. I needed backup.

SIDEBAR

When we'd left Fort McMurray in 2008, we did it with the intention that Mike would have to commute for eight months until his retention contract at work had been fulfilled. We figured that would give us some time to make some business connections in Red Deer, and that Mike would be able to get a job no problem. We had moved to Red Deer in August, and that fall, a recession hit. Leaving a secure job where Mike had been for many years was not a good idea, so we made the decision to continue with the commuter lifestyle, one that is very common for people living in the Red Deer region.

We justified the commuting at the beginning with things like: "Mike doesn't see the kids when he is working anyway. He is gone to work before they wake up and they're asleep before he gets home." The reality was that life had to go on when he was away, and he missed out on a lot of family life. I struggled to run the show by myself, and our life was in a constant state of transition. Things were done one way when he was away, but then I had to give up that control and authority when he came home. There was always a battle and power struggle on his first day home, and we typically spent the day bickering at each other. It was like clockwork. It was a little easier when the kids were small and we still had "control", but once they moved toward adolescence, it was a different ball game altogether.

I will never, ever again support the idea of commuting in that way. Families are stronger together. It is unfair to insist that one member of the family live away from the rest in order to have a better quality of life. The reality of oil-patch commuting, where the oil-patch worker lives away from the family during his or her "days on" cycle, really only works well for those couples that don't really like each other and crave the space. I can guarantee that your marriage and family will suffer in the work-away lifestyle. It may not happen right away, but you will have regrets over the damage done, or the feelings your kids grow up with, feeling like dad was not there for them.

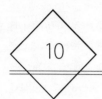

A LEAP OF FAITH

A nd so, after the beetle incident, the decision was made to go to Fort McMurray for the summer. Both our houses were vacant and my contract position in Olds ended up fizzling out to nothing. There was nothing to keep us in Olds. Our accommodations were not working anymore, the job didn't work out, and we felt torn. God had called us to Olds - but for only a few months? I struggled with this decision. The evening we were to leave for Fort McMurray, we met all of the *BFC* at Tim Hortons for a visit and send-off. After we said our goodbyes and were driving away, for whatever reason, I was overcome with a sense of peace. I was going into the unknown, but there was such a strong confidence in the direction we were heading. In that moment, everything was okay.

As we settled back in to Fort McMurray, we were very short on cash. I sometimes wondered where/how I'd get my next meal. We had to get assistance from the church for groceries. With only Mike's income and two houses worth of expenses, we were a family of four living on $200 a month. Most days, I only ate once, in order to make sure the kids were fed. We made the sacrifice to buy a month family pass to MacDonald Island, a huge recreation facility in Fort Mac, where we went swimming almost every day. We got library memberships and occupied ourselves with all kinds of books and movies.

The house was empty, as in unfurnished. We were sitting on lawn chairs and coolers. All of our stuff was in Red Deer, but we were only planning to stay for the summer. We were able to scrape together some furniture from a Facebook group called "Too Good to Dump". We had some of our camping dishes, and it definitely felt like were camping in our house. I hated it. I didn't feel settled or at home. There were no pictures on the walls nor any of my vintage dishes around.

Kaci got a job at Dairy Queen for the summer, and I started working at David's Tea. I didn't want to use any of my connection to get a job in my field if we were only going to stay for the summer, but we needed money desperately, so working retail wouldn't be much, but it would be better than nothing.

We started attending our old church, McMurray Gospel Assembly. Mike had grown up attending this church. It was also the one in which we were married, and both the kids had been dedicated there as babies. Fort McMurray is a place in constant transition. People are always coming and going. The first Sunday we attended, I realized I only recognized about 10% of the people. The place had changed a lot over the five years we'd been away.

I could see Kaci starting to make bad choices again. We were fighting with her a lot. Over the summer, we had a confrontation with her that resulted in the police being called. She was taken to a youth shelter. Every Sunday, I would go to church, and go up for prayer. I couldn't believe this was happening again. My world was crumbling around me, and as strong as I thought I had become from the last eight months, I still found myself slipping back into hopelessness. While at the front of the church yet again, asking for prayer for my family, I met Brian and Dianalee. They prayed with me, and spoke life and hope into our situation. We all felt a connection, and they asked if we could get together. I felt that somehow they needed to be a part of our journey, and I was right - they have come to play a significant role in our lives.

Every Sunday was the same thing: lots of crying. I felt like church was only place I didn't have to be strong and put on a front. I could be broken and raw there, and it was a place to find healing. We reconnected with Pastors Phil and Linda. They had raised five kids and all of them were alive and well. Their insight proved very valuable; they described the relationship with a teenager as a very delicate dance. There had to be the right mix of boundaries and freedom, or they could choose to walk out and the parents would then lose any opportunity to parent and guide them. They also advised us to make sure to pray like crazy. Great advice!

By the first week in August there had been few showings on each of the houses, and we needed to figure out a plan. We couldn't be in limbo come fall, as the kids would need to be registered in school somewhere. Neither of the kids were happy to be in Fort McMurray, and both wanted to go back to Red Deer. Hey, let's face it, I wanted to be back in Red Deer, too! I missed my friends and support system, but Red Deer was not an option. Mike and I decided that we would stay in Fort McMurray. It was the only way for us to be together as a family, and things were starting to go sour with Kaci again. I wouldn't be able to deal with things on my own.

Once we made the decision to stay, I went and found a job at the United Way, and we made plans for Mike to go down to Red Deer on the long weekend in September to get our stuff. It turned out that all of that packing I'd done before the move to the farm, in preparation for who-knows-what, was a big blessing.

Kaci had relapsed over the summer, and in August, we found drugs in her bag. The ensuing conflict resulted in her attempting to bolt, and me physically restraining her. I had learned that no judge in the world would let an assault charge stand on a parent that was trying to prevent their child from leaving. Kaci ended up at a local youth shelter for five days, while we tried to cool off and figure out how to get through these teenage years.

I was so happy, that weekend in September, to see the moving truck roll up with all of our stuff. We had not anticipated moving back, and our Fort McMurray house was 1000 square feet smaller than our Red Deer house. There was no way that all of that stuff was going to fit into our small place. As each box was opened, nearly half of its contents went out to the garage to be sold in a garage sale. As hard as this was, it was also very freeing. Learning to live with less is a great lesson for everyone.

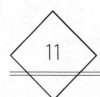

11

MUSIC: A SOURCE OF HOPE

God uses so many different mediums and means to speak, guide and encourage us in tough times. I had a co-worker at the church in Red Deer named Deanna, who shared during our staff devotional time the impact that a certain song had during some pretty dark days in her life. She played the song "Build us Back" by The Newsboys. It would be a song that would get me through some dark places. The song went like this...

We've been crumbled, we've been crushed
City walls have turned to dust
Broken hands and blistered feet
We walk for miles to find relief

When the thief takes, when our hopes cave
You build us back
You build us back

When the earth shakes, when the world breaks
You build us back
You build us back

We are scared, we are poor
All our safety nets are torn
We've been humbled to our knees
From these ruins, we believe

When the thief takes, when our hopes cave
You build us back
You build us back

When the earth shakes, when the world breaks
You build us back
You build us back

Redeemer, redeem us
Restorer, restore us
Oh build us back
Though the mountains be shaken, the hills be removed[1]
Your unfailing love remains
After all that's been taken, Your promise, still sacred
You build us back with precious stones

When the thief takes, when our hopes cave
You build us back
You build us back

When the earth shakes, when the world breaks
You build us back
You build us back

I remember laying on my bed, crying, with my phone on my chest, listening to this song and the promise and hope it gave me at such a dark time. It was the hardest thing I ever did - declaring victory over my darkness, when everything around me said otherwise. It was trusting in something I could feel, but not see.

Every time we went to church, the depth of the words we were singing would hit me like a ton of bricks. I wondered if anyone else there understood the importance of declaring victory, or if they were just singing words and critiquing how well the band played that day. I would pray, sing, worship, cry. I had no choice but to cling to the hope and promises that were in those words. Another song that stood out, that I felt in a way was my promise, was **Cornerstone** by Hillsong.

Cornerstone Lyrics

My hope is built on nothing less
Than Jesus blood and righteousness
I dare not trust the sweetest frame
But wholly trust in Jesus name

My hope is built on nothing less
Than Jesus blood and righteousness
I dare not trust the sweetest frame
But wholly trust in Jesus name

Christ alone; cornerstone
Weak made strong; in the Saviour's love
Through the storm, He is Lord
Lord of all

When Darkness seems to hide His face
I rest on His unchanging grace
In every high and stormy gale
My anchor holds within the veil
My anchor holds within the veil

Christ alone; cornerstone
Weak made strong; in the Saviour's love
Through the storm, He is Lord
Lord of all
He is Lord
Lord of all

Christ alone
Christ alone; cornerstone
Weak made strong; in the Saviour's love
Through the storm, He is Lord
Lord of all

Christ alone; cornerstone
Weak made strong; in the Saviour's love
Through the storm, He is Lord
Lord of all

When He shall come with trumpet sound,
Oh, may I then in Him be found;
Dressed in His righteousness alone,
Faultless stand before the throne.²

Over the last few years, that song has touched my heart many times. When we attended my dad's sixtieth birthday celebration, Kaci wanted to sing a song for my dad. As we stood in the stairwell of the legion, Kaci started to sing that song with the voice of an angel. I was overcome with emotion. It was as if God whispered to me, "Although this story isn't done, the lyrics are in your girl's heart, and she will mean them one day." God doesn't do a half job. He is faithful to complete the work He has started in Kaci. I have absolute confidence that, after this season, Kaci *will* serve the Lord again whole heartedly, on her own terms. Her relationship with God will look different than mine, and that's okay.

It turns out that our friend Brian Walrond has a really cool talent, writing what he calls "Prophetic Prose". His albums are spoken word put to music and are absolutely incredible. To be honest, after listening to his album "Beyond Me", I really thought that a couple of songs were written *for me*! That is the beauty of the lyrics God gives him. These songs meet people where they are at in their brokenness, and offer hope.

We were visiting with Brian and Dianalee, and the prose *"What a difference a year makes"* came up in conversation. As I reflected on the journey of the last few years, that statement rang so true. What a difference a year makes. Year after year, I could look back and see the slow but steady progress, with Kaci finding herself again. Although we are not yet finished this season, we are light years away from where we were a year ago.

What a Difference a Year Makes
From the time you felt the rumble and the ground shake.
And then you took that tumble felt your heart break,
And now your heart aches and the wound runs so deep that your heart hates.
And life happened to you and left you numb. And now you obsess on what you shouldn't or should have done.
Or maybe you're the one that did something dumb,
But whatever happened to you, it left you stunned.
And as the storm clouds come they will surely pass.
I don't have a crystal ball to tell you how long it lasts.
For some it goes slow man and for others fast, but I know there's hope that's why I ask, "What a difference a year makes?"
I know it takes time, but really, how long should time take in the midst of the pain?
It's hard not to lose faith because you need grace,
But if you respond right, it'll be worth the wait.
As the numbing fades and you begin to feel, drop your masks, face yourself man, and get real.
I know you got your pride, but it's time to yield.
And you need to forgive if you wanna heal. It takes time to realize that emotions lie,
And when you thought it was over, still you haven't died and just when you thought you've lost it all still God provides,

I share this prose with you, to help you come alive. What a difference a year makes,
things are getting better, but you still ache.
You thought you were judged, but you found grace.
And destructive patterns in your life are being replaced,
what a difference a year makes.
The bitterness of life's got a new taste, every day's a new day with a new slate.
And life is not a sprint, but a long race so try to keep pace and 12 months from today you could be in a new place.
What a difference a year makes.

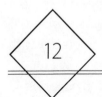

12

FEAR

As moms, I think we often live in fear pretty much 24/7. From the time we discover we are pregnant, we are in a constant state of anxiety over all of the "what ifs" that could possibly go wrong. The momma bear instincts kick in, and every choice and decision we make from birth onward is for the betterment of our children, but in truth, those decisions are our way of controlling our environment and trying to keep everything "right" in our world.

When I was a young parent, my dad would frequently spend time reflecting on his life as a parent. He would say to me, like a broken record, "You have to give up control to have influence." He would repeat this every time we would visit together, and after a while, it got seriously annoying. This statement, though, would later come to have a huge impact on our lives. One lesson that I was to learn in all of this was the importance of giving up and surrendering my control over my life and Kaci's life. It was not mine to control. I tried - boy, did I try! The rebellion only escalated.

Years ago, I bought the book *The Power of a Praying Parent* by Stormie Omartian. The funny thing is that I didn't read the whole thing when I bought it, but when I picked it up and started reading it in this season, I was struck by the level of fear in which she lived. Her prayers for her kids were completely rooted in fear. I am not knocking her for that - we all have our struggles; It was just something I observed and noted. My take away from that book was that before I could effectively pray for my kids, I needed to first surrender my fear. I needed to first trust my Father with my kids. My prayers for my kids could not and should not be rooted in fear.

One day I had an epiphany of sorts that really helped me understand better why I needed to give up trying to control Kaci, and all those around me, and focus on those things I could do something about. This was the epiphany:

"Control, at its root, is fear. Fear is the opposite of trust. Fear can be rooted in jealousy, perfectionism, feelings of judgement, being alone and the list goes on. But whatever it is, it is still FEAR. Until we learn the reasons for fear we can never release control. This may be of a child or spouse or co-worker. Security in who we are can only come from trust. Until we have that we will be broken and so will all the relationships we have. Everyone loses when we try to control."

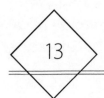

13

BOUNDARIES

As the kids were growing up, we set boundaries with them. Whether it was where in the neighborhood they could play, or how late they could stay up; they had boundaries. After Kaci came home from *Venture*, she was with us for a few months and then left. The first time she left, it was for three months. During that time, we pleaded with her to come home every time she made contact. She finally did come home, for three weeks, and then left again, this time for five months. Those nine months were the ugliest in our lives.

Kaci was homeless, couch surfing and using every drug she could get her hands on. Every ugly thing the world has to offer that could happen to her, did. After consulting with *Venture*, we set some boundaries with her. We told her that we loved her and wanted her to be part of the family, but that she was no longer welcome in our home, unless she would get sober & go back to school. She was not interested in either of those things, and stayed away.

Through this ordeal, I have learned that when someone is truly homeless, there is no possible way they can work or go to school.

They are struggling all day, every day, to make a plan for where to sleep at night, and that takes all their time and energy.

A roof over one's head is such a basic need and that is the reason why many communities embrace a "Housing First" model when dealing with people who are homeless. Nothing else can come together until someone has a home. They can't work on their addictions or the relationships in their life until they have a place to lay their head at night.

In order to bring some stability and sanity to our home, we felt we'd had to set a boundary with Kaci. Every day, we were in crisis. It was constant. Brody needed more than what we were offering, and it wasn't until we set those boundaries with Kaci that we were able to have a little bit of 'normal.'

Kaci finally came home in the summer, and was home for almost three months. I truly believed that when she came home that this was it – she was home for good, and things would improve. Although she had quit all of the hard drugs, she was still smoking weed every day, behind our backs. When she left again that fall, we gave her a few days to cool off. She was feeling like the weight of having to go to school was too much. Those few days away from home turned into three weeks. Finally, we decided it was time to set a hard boundary with her.

Mike had got to the hard line place way before I did. It really comes down to a place of self-preservation. I was living in constant fear, worrying about all of the horrible "what ifs" that for some reason well-meaning people felt the need to "educate" me on the dangers Kaci faced. We were challenged a lot by people who didn't agree with how we were handling things, because they felt our boundaries were potentially putting Kaci at risk.

They would say things like: "She's a pretty girl. Something bad might happen if she can't come home."

I felt like yelling: "No kidding! Duh – like as if I didn't know that!"

This was where I had to do what was the hardest thing ever: I had to let go. Think about that for a second. I had to let her go, to give her back to God. Like that whole baby dedication thing, but this time it was for real! I literally had to place her in God's hands and trust that His plans and purposes for her were good. I had to surrender everything I wanted for her - including all of my hopes and dreams for her and even my desire for her safety - and all I was allowed to pray was, "God, please spare her life!" Of course I wanted to pray things like: "Please don't let her get raped or pregnant or overdose or beaten or or or or or or….." But God showed me that by doing that, I was tying His hands. Our Father in Heaven does honor the prayers of parents. But there are times that we truly get in the way of what needs to happen because of our own - can you guess? Fear!

The day after my birthday, I was texting with my friend Sandey. She and her husband Dave are close friends of ours from the *BFC* chapter in Olds. Sandey and Dave had walked this path with their daughter years before, and, in an act of obedience, she lovingly and firmly sent me a message that changed my perspective, and gave me so much peace. The message went like this:

"You need to surrender and be obedient, Beth, to the Lord in this. LET. HER. GO. Kaci is not your daughter. She is borrowed to you. Do you not think that God doesn't know how to take care of HIS children? Of course he does. We as parents often get in the way of something real, deep that HE wants to do with our own kids. I don't say this lightly my sweet sister… I understand this and it is

not easy and it does hurt and is not fair! But God IS fair, He heals your raw pain and will make an easier path for you when we completely, totally surrender.

Praise and worship the Lord for and in everything, Beth. It is that agonizing, unfelt, sacrificial praise that sets you free from Kaci and begins the magical answers. You can and will be able to do this, Beth… you and Mike together and you as a daughter. Jeremiah 29:11-14."

And so I did it. Totally broken, I told Kaci that we were done. I told her we loved her and that if she chose not to come home, she would no longer have a bedroom at our house. She would always be welcome for a meal, or could sleep on the couch, but we would no longer keep her room. During the three weeks she had been home it had been her fifteenth birthday, and we had renovated her room in the hopes she would feel at home and stay, but that did not work out very well. I had packed up all of her belongings, but the room remained; never touched. It was time to breathe some life back into our home and make use of that room again.

I would say that the boundaries thing is always the hardest part: doing what needs to be done, not what I *feel* needs to be done. It takes a lot of strength to stand your ground and not buckle under the pressure. Many fights happened between Mike and me because I would buckle under Kaci's manipulation. The darkest times in our marriage came from fighting over what to do about Kaci. We seldom agreed. I lived in fear – a lot. I can see now how families are torn apart and people divorce over the death or addictions with children.

I have, since that season, met dozens of recovering addicts whom God has strategically placed in my life. One lady said to me that her parents enabled her, and that she never really had a reason to change. They too lived in fear, and that fear is what drove them to give her money, food, a place, a cell phone and whatever else she asked for because they wanted her to be safe. Really, though, it was to satisfy their own fears and not do what they needed to do to break the cycle. I don't pretend for a minute to claim that I have this addiction thing all figured out, but what I can tell you is that Kaci now understands real love, and that is not always jumping when she says jump. She has a great amount of respect for us, and will tell anyone that she has the best parents in the world.

I was always afraid that she would hate me. Boy, did she hate me… but that does change. Now there is respect, and Kaci knows where she stands. I love her no matter what. I may not agree with her choices but she knows that won't change my love for her.

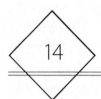

14

OUR CALLING

I have learned that it is nobody's job to make you happy... not your spouse, or kids, or friends. There are many days that I am not happy, but that is my choice. Happiness is a choice. Choosing to bloom where you are planted, even if you don't want to be there, is a choice. I may not like where I am, even though I know it is exactly where God wants me, but I am learning every day to choose happiness for myself. Some days I do better than others. Some days, I just want to hide under the blankets, but I choose to get up and thank God for the air in my lungs and remind myself of all I have, and try not to focus on what I have lost or don't have.

I say all that to say that Fort McMurray was and is the last place on earth that I would like to be living. I know many Christians who are fearful that if they surrender their lives to Christ that he may ask them to go be a missionary in Africa or something equally terrible. Well, Fort McMurray is my Africa. I don't say that because Fort McMurray is a horrible place. Contrary to what you may think or have heard or read, it is a beautiful place and a wonderful community. However, for me personally, it is a struggle, mainly because of its distance from my family and the mountains. But I know that I know that I know that we are here for a real purpose and until that purpose is accomplished, this is where we will stay.

Back to the missionary bit. Going to another country is very challenging. But when God calls you, he equips you. I would say, though, that it is more difficult to go back to your home town with people that you grew up with, to those people who saw you struggle through the teenage years. That has been our reality. Mike grew up in Fort McMurray. He is an anomaly, actually, since most people come here from somewhere else. Now, to see Mike, you would/could be frightened to death or at least a little intimidated by his appearance. He is, in every sense of the word, a "Biker": Big, Bald, Beard, and tattooed. Biker. But it only takes a minute of talking to Mike to see that he is actually a big softy that cares deeply for people. He loves people, but he's a quiet guy, and not what most would necessarily see as a dynamic leader. He hates public speaking, and doesn't like to be the center of attention, which is good for us, because I am the loud one and have had many leadership positions.

We were back in Fort McMurray for nearly six months when Mike started getting approached by different guys, some believers, some not, and one guy who went to high school with him, all saying that he should start a *BFC* chapter up in Fort Mac. Over the course of a couple of weeks, half a dozen guys all said the same thing to him. He resisted. I told him to pray about it; maybe this was the reason we were back! Mike has never seen himself as a leader. He loves to be involved with things, but has always been more of a behind-the-scenes guy. After a couple of weeks, Mike surrendered his will to God's, and within a short period of time

Bikers for Christ Wood Buffalo was born. Mike, of course, became the Chapter Elder.

I was, and still am, so proud of him for laying down his fear and saying, "Your will, Lord, not mine." He started a men's biker bible study that now meets every week, and we have had up to nineteen guys crammed into our living room. We have had to move the bible study to the garage and now 30+ men are showing up every week. The guys that come are not your typical "church going, men's ministry" kind of guys. They are guys with a history of pain, addiction, violence, and they all have amazing stories of redemption through faith. Mike and I both agree that this **BFC** ministry is not a numbers game. We currently sit at six members, myself included. If we only have six forever, that is okay. The priority is to reach out to the other bike clubs - outlaw and otherwise - and offer friendship, prayer and support wherever needed.

We recently "patched in" a hang-around (you'll have to google what that means – it's a biker term). We invited members of another motorcycle club to join us. After the event was over, text messages came in from people who'd attended saying how welcome they all felt. The members have even reached out, asking for prayer for injured members. These guys would never set foot in a church or ask for prayer, but Mike is getting requests like this on a regular basis.

Every call to visit someone in the hospital, or to pray for a struggling brother, affirms in my heart we are exactly where we are supposed to be. For once, my role is now behind the scenes and Mike's is front and center. I pray for the group all the time and try to be as understanding as I can when Mike is gone for weekends at a time to different events, or on his phone all night encouraging his brothers and anyone else that may call.

I trust that this season here will accomplish all God has for us and someday, Lord willing, I will be able to return closer to the mountains.

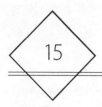

15

GRIEF

I think it was Madonna who had a song that says: *"Time goes by so slowly."* That is a very true statement. As we weathered the storm, I came to a point where I was so empty, so lonely, and felt like I could not go on. I chose to isolate myself from what I felt were shallow conversations and from the people who had them, as my daily reality was so drastically different from everyone else's. This decision, though I did not see it as a "decision" at the time, was a double edged sword. Not only did I feel like I was walking through this alone, but I also put a lot of pressure – in fact, way too much pressure - on Mike to fill the emotional needs I had that were not being filled through friendships.

When Kaci had walked out that last time, after only being home three months, I became a basket case of sorts. Crying all the time… in public, at the doctor's office, everywhere.

Always on the verge of tears. It was at this point I finally decided I needed to get help. I went to an *Employee and Family Assistance Program (EFAP)* counselor through Mike's work, and she and I clicked instantly. Her name was Juanita. She was from South Africa and had grown up in a family with siblings who struggled with addictions. Her own son also had this struggle. I felt like she "got" me. Our sessions were different all the time. Some good, some really ugly - like, snot-and-mascara-all-over-my-face ugly, but she listened and never judged, and pushed me when I needed pushing. I appreciated that she was tough enough to call me out on those things that I needed to be called out on, and always challenged me to be kind to myself.

About six months in she said something to me that devastated me, and yet put a face and name to what I could not identify. She said to me that every time I came to see her, whether I was doing well or not, there was a profound sadness in my eyes that was always there. Every time. This was exactly what I had been feeling for the last few years. Not a depression of sorts, but a cloud of profound sadness that was an unseen and unwelcomed guest in my every day. Coffee with friends? It was there. Alone time with Mike? It was there. I couldn't shake it. It was as though I had experienced a death I could not identify and yet every day the pain was there. Profound Sadness, she called it… an ever-present reminder of all I had given up and lost.

Juanita challenged me to take some time to grieve over what I had given up, and what I felt I had lost through this whole thing. That was my homework: to cry for those things. I told her jokingly that I was going to throw her under the bus if Mike said anything about me crying for homework.

I went home and mulled this over. Within a few days, I opened up a new journal and started to write. I made a list of all of the things that I felt I had given up or lost through these last two years. Maybe it seems slightly ridiculous to grieve some of these things, but I did. The list was long, but reflected the loss I felt.

I missed what was supposed to be my "forever home"

I missed that my kids would never be able to say "I grew up on Langford Crescent"

I missed my church in Red Deer (Living Stones)

I missed my paved bike paths

I missed going to the Saturday farmers market

I missed Kevin & Becky and their Cool Beans Bus Coffee shop

I missed buying Humble Hummus from Jason

I missed my friend Chris and going to the home show every year

I missed going for noodles with Amy

I missed cutting my grass and sitting in my hot tub

I really missed my community gardens I had established

I missed talking politics with my friend Danielle

I missed running into my buddy Jennifer at the grocery store and seeing her excitement about her coupons

I missed snow shoeing with my friend Kim & talking life with my friend Shelley… no masks or pretending… just authentic friendship

I missed being close to the mountains and going on day trips to Bass Pro or to Canmore for my anniversary

I missed Kaci

I missed being her mom, being together, baking cookies or doing art or watching her dance

I missed her purity and innocent way she loved life

I missed listening to her sing

I missed camping as a family when it was not stressful and we could just "be" together

Oh the things I ached for. I asked myself if the Profound Sadness would ever leave.

I found out a few days later. The pressure that had been building between Mike and me, as I looked to him to be my "everything", finally came to a head when I got upset about him going away for a weekend. I had pushed him to a place that he wanted to give up *BFC*, sell his motorcycle and walk away from all of it. If I couldn't be supportive, then he wanted nothing to do with it. This very difficult twenty-four hours was a huge wake up call for me. I had to acknowledge that I had used Mike to fill that void and had not been a very good wife in the process; another hard pill to swallow. I was getting in the way of what God wanted to do through us in Fort McMurray. Setting up a *Bikers for Christ* chapter in Fort McMurray was the reason why we had been sent here; I knew that. Although my role was not to be the leader, my role was and is just as important as Mike's. A calling like *BFC* is not one that can be done successfully without the love, support and calling by the spouses of the members. It's a team calling, with very different roles. To think that I was getting in the way of that, even as I write this, makes me cringe.

Our battle lasted two days. The second day I only made it to lunch and left work. I drove out to Gregoire Lake and found a somewhat secluded area near a boat launch. I was so emotional and fearful that this could be the end of our marriage. I was also still trying to figure out how to be released from the Profound Sadness. I sat in my car looking at the lake through the trees, and reread the list I had made of all the things I felt I lost. It was then that the tears came and I finally got the time and space to cry for me… to cry over all I felt I had lost, and to cry for what would never be. When I was done and there was half a box of Kleenex on the seat beside me, I laid my seat back with a blanket from my car and had a nap. The crying had left me so exhausted I did not have the strength or energy to drive, or even to get out of the car. The nap was enough to rejuvenate me, so I grabbed my journal and the blanket and went down to the lake. For the next hour I sat there, wrote my thoughts in a journal and messaged Mike, begging for his forgiveness. It was an ugly twenty-four hours, but very necessary, as it turned out, to my healing and moving forward.

I left the Profound Sadness on the Shore of Gregoire Lake that day. It hasn't reappeared, and I feel that I can start moving forward with my life, like a cut that has healed but scarred. Healed, but forever changed in appearance.

FOR EVERYTHING A SEASON

The positive side of distancing myself from shallowness was that I made a conscious decision to "get a life" and start exploring some new hobbies and interests. I did so alone. People would often comment how awesome it was that I wasn't sitting around waiting for life to happen or for someone to come to me to do something fun - I was actually taking initiative to do it myself. This was the way I chose to fill myself, take back some control of my life, and choose my response to my circumstances. Now, I know that ultimately I have no control over my life. I have solely given that over to God to manage and navigate as he sees fit; but still, I have choices to make.

Choosing my response to this season meant choosing to pour into *me*, and purposely exploring some new interests. These interests took some pressure off of Mike, and even Brody, for that matter. As we moved into the season on teenage-dom, I had to realize that my role with Brody and Kaci was now of more of an advisor and prayer partner than anything else. I could see my time with them slipping away. And where the teenage years are the testing ground for adulthood, the teenage years - for the parents - is the learning to be an individual again, and not make your kids miserable by trying to spend every waking minute with them. With this in mind and my newfound spare time, I made some choices:

I love to swim. I grew up in swim club, and really missed it. I used to swim with my aunt Rochelle in Red Deer but had quit some time ago. I now started taking Saturday mornings, before Brody was even awake, and going to swim 1 km, and then do a deep water aqua fit class. This left me refreshed, and gave a sense of accomplishment.

I took up running. I am soooo not a runner! To get some sanity back and feel good about myself, I signed up for 4 races over a spring/summer. The races were goals, to keep me motivated. I ran three times a week with a "learn to run" program, and struggled with nearly every run. There were only a handful of times where I felt sheer elation while running, but this was something I wanted for myself, so I persisted. Never having a running partner; just me and my playlist.

I discovered coloring for adults and bought a dozen different books. Since I had given up TV a year or so prior, I had all kinds of time to pour myself into things that actually mattered, or added value. I have learned that TV and social media add very little value to one's life, and they can suck life out of you instead of adding to it. Television especially sucks us into the world's definition of value and success and acquiring "things"; things that only bring short term fulfillment and not long term gain, things that rob us of living, things that take up time, storing, cleaning and rearranging. I didn't always understand the bible phrase about being "in the world but not of it" until we moved back to Fort McMurray. For me, that has meant rejecting most media and instead focussing my time and energies on other things. I still follow the news but instead of checking it five times a day, it's more like once or twice a week.

I took up shooting. This was something completely out of character for me! All of my friends and family were actually shocked. I had grown up with a father who was an avid hunter and outdoorsmen, but it was not something in which I had ever been remotely interested. After my dad bought Brody a little .22 for gopher hunting, I realized that he would never get to use it, as nobody in our house had their *Possession & Acquisition License (PAL)*. I decided that I wanted Brody to have as many positive outlets as possible, considering the impact everything had on him, so without saying anything to Mike, I registered for my *PAL* course. Of course, upon hearing of my course registration, Mike could not let me get my *PAL* before him! He took the course the weekend before me. In early spring, I got to go to Edmonton, take a weekend with my dad and go gun shopping. It was the first time since I was a kid that we had ever spent together alone. He'd been waiting my whole life for me to say I wanted a gun, so he jumped at the chance. Although I did agree to go hunting with him once (like as if freezing in a field in November in the hopes of getting a deer is any fun), I was more drawn to purchasing a hand gun… totally weird. I named my gun "Stella". Funny, right? I love going on dates to the gun range and shooting at the targets with Stella. In some weird way, this was very empowering; perhaps because the thought of handing a firearm totally terrified me, and building the confidence to go there alone and learn a new skill that was completely foreign to me was very exhilarating. It brought a whole new meaning to that adage: "Do one thing every day that scares you". The members of the gun club were very helpful in teaching me all I needed to know.

I made time to ride my bike. I had purchased my dream bicycle almost five years previous. I loved my bike so much that I named her Eleanor, and took her everywhere around Red Deer. Then I left her for two whole summers, being too wrapped up in the cares of life to get out and smell the roses. Now I try to get out every week. Oh the joy I get from bike riding!

I went to school. Yup. I finally got to go to college. They say that education in Canada is accessible to everyone, but that is, in fact, not true; there are situations that make it impossible for a person to get an education. When I was young, that was the case. But after moving back to Fort McMurray, I felt like it was time. Applying was terrifying, but getting accepted was awesome. I am working on a Human Resources Management Certificate. It's sometimes weird, being in class with nineteen-year-olds, but it means so much for me to be there. I've waited my whole life for this. Aside from an apocalyptic event, which we have so far avoided, nothing keeps me from going to class. It's going to take me awhile to finish, since I'm only taking one course per semester, but at least I am working towards a goal and if all goes as planned, Kaci and I could graduate the same time. I have promised her that if she can graduate on time, I will take her backpacking in New Zealand. Whether she graduates on time or not, I will be going on this trip! I hold that as a carrot in front of her in the hopes that she will choose to go back to school. I keep praying this will happen.

But for now, this is now is the season of self-discovery and personal healing.

17

ANSWERED PRAYERS

Timing is everything. We pray, and sometimes we get a response, and sometimes we have to wait. Sometimes the answer isn't what we wanted. This could be the longest chapter in the book, but I want to highlight some of the significant things that prayer did for us during this time. I believe that prayer truly is what kept Kaci alive through her darkest times. When she was at the end of herself, and wanted to end her life, it was prayer, and the Holy Spirit, intervening and preventing her from following through. When I placed Kaci at the feet of God, giving her to him to look out for and take care of, I felt in my spirit that I was not to pray for her for a few weeks; all I needed to do was trust. During this period, we got random messages from other people who said they felt that they needed to pray for her. We later found out that Kaci's life had been in danger during our time of trusting, but that the prayers of friends and family sustained us, and protected Kaci.

One Sunday before Christmas, we experienced a miracle of sorts. Kaci, who was, at this point, combining living in her car and couch surfing, showed up to church. I was shocked. This, in itself, was a miracle. The second miracle came when she went up for prayer. All I could do was weep and try to sing. It was a sight I will remember the rest of my life. At the time, I did not know why Kaci went up for prayer, but I soon found out. Kaci said she felt the presence of the Lord so strongly that she had to leave the service and go outside for a cigarette, just to relieve the intensity. I found this quite humorous, actually.

When she came back in, I just had to speak to her and find out what was going on. Kaci's biological father had contacted me that very morning, after no contact in thirteen years. He had never met Kaci, and, through his mother, had learned that Kaci wanted to meet him. That is what she had come to church to pray about: that she would get to meet him. When I told her in the lobby about the call and his desire to meet her, she hugged me and thanked me, and I was able to tell her that God knows and does answer our prayers, even sometimes before we pray them.

Kaci had been off hard drugs for nearly a year, but suffered terribly with anxiety. She would self-medicate with marijuana, to settle her mind. Marijuana works well to chill a person out in the moment, but also aggravates anxiety overall, and so a vicious cycle is created. We often had heated debates over her marijuana use, with me challenging her to think about the big picture.

She would say things like, "Nobody has ever died from a marijuana overdose!"

I would reply back, "Perhaps nobody has ever died from it, but can you tell me that what you are doing right now is really living?"

Her anxiety was so out of control that she could not go to school, be left alone, or keep a job. I sent her a few articles about anxiety and marijuana use and explained my belief that, until she chose something else for her life, that living with anxiety would be a daily thing, and she would not be able to move ahead and get her life back on track. A few weeks went by, and as I made my bed before work one morning, I prayed that Kaci would see that all of these things that she was using to fill the void were cheap imitations and would ultimately lead her nowhere.

The same day, I got a text message from Kaci. She asked me to make an appointment at the doctor so she could get some anti-anxiety medication, and told me she was going to quit smoking weed. BAM!

Another time, Kaci messaged me while I was at church, freaking out about a situation involving lost keys. I told her I was going up to get prayer. At the front of the church, I pleaded with God for mercy for the situation. A lady sitting beside me at church could see I was visibly shaken, as I was sitting there crying and praying. She leaned over, placed her hand on my shoulder and prayed for Kaci. She then had a word for me.

She said, "You have shared your testimony about your daughter before. The God that protected her before is the same today as he was then, and he will accomplish his plans and purposes for your daughter." What a word of encouragement!

Within minutes, there was a message back from Kaci, saying that the situation had been resolved without major consequences and Kaci's living arrangements would not be threatened, which had been a possibility. This was exactly what I had prayed, and I was once again reminded that God knows and cares about our every need.

I had been taught a few years earlier by Pastor Paul to journal my prayers. We pray for a lot of things, and if you have a memory like mine, well… I forget a lot of what I pray about, so I started writing out my prayers and then looking back every so often to reflect and thank God for his answers. It is amazing how faith-building it is to see and be reminded that God is still present and active in all of our situations.

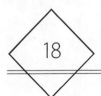

18

PAIN THAT HEALS

At New Year's one year, I felt very strongly that I was to share at that service about what God was doing in our lives. The church was looking for people who would be willing to share and encourage others as we ushered into the New Year. I was nervous, as this would be the first time that I would publically share what we had been walking through.

This is a little bit of what I shared that evening.

"Towards the end of 2012 I was working at a church in Red Deer. As a staff team, we were seeking the Lord and were encouraged to ask God if there may be a theme or word for the New Year. My word was Restoration. I wrote it on my white board, excited for what 2013 may hold. Little did I know that 2013 and 2014 would be the hardest years of my life.

Within weeks of getting this word, the bottom of my life fell out. Our daughter Kaci had turned 13 that year and, struggling to fit in, she got involved in drugs. The next 2 years would see us seeking God and going to extreme lengths to try and help her: police officers, court rooms, Treatment Centres, out of province visits, moving back to Fort McMurray, meetings with our MLA, & Youth Advocates.

She would live with us and then be gone for months at a time and come home only to turn around and leave again. The roller coaster of fear and emotions felt all consuming at times. For me this was some real "rubber hits the spiritual road". Either God was real or he wasn't and if he was then he was my only hope in keeping my daughter alive. When my situation looked like it was completely hopeless I had to stand on God's promises for mine and Kaci's life. 2 specific scriptures I clung to during this were:

Jeremiah 29:11 For I know the plans I have for you," declares the Lord, "plans to prosper you and not to harm you, plans to give you hope and a future.

Romans 8:28 And we know that in all things God works for the good of those who love him, who[a] have been called according to his purpose.

The week that everything fell apart Mike and I were at church and God gave us a verse that we had painted for our bedroom as a constant reminder.

2 Corinthians 12:9 But he said to me, "My grace is sufficient for you, for my power is made perfect in weakness." Therefore I will boast all the more gladly about my weaknesses, so that Christ's power may rest on me.

Restoration and healing comes in many forms. Although it was hard to see it at the time I can look back now and see restoration all over this.

1. The relationship with a family friend, with whom we'd had a falling out a few years prior, was restored.

2. Our family is back under one roof again full time as Mike no longer commutes.

3. I have been able to heal from my past with Kaci's father and Kaci is able to fit that piece of the puzzle of her life together.

4. We left our Bikers for Christ family in Olds and grieved losing our support system, and this past year, Bikers for Christ Wood Buffalo was birthed, out of a dark place and a surrender to God's plans for us.

This journey is still far from over for us but I know without a shadow of a doubt that Kaci is in the palm of my Father's hand and that He does not finish something half way. I know I will see her serving Christ again and will have a crazy testimony.

I want to wrap up by reading Psalm 23 from *The Message* as an encouragement to those going through tough times right now:

Psalm 23, The Message (MSG)

A David Psalm

23 ¹⁻³ GOD, my shepherd!
    I don't need a thing.
You have bedded me down in lush meadows,
    you find me quiet pools to drink from.
True to your word,
    you let me catch my breath

and send me in the right direction.
⁴ Even when the way goes through
   Death Valley,
I'm not afraid
   when you walk at my side.
Your trusty shepherd's crook
   makes me feel secure.

⁵ You serve me a six-course dinner
   right in front of my enemies.
You revive my drooping head;
   my cup brims with blessing.

⁶ Your beauty and love chase after me
   every day of my life.
I'm back home in the house of GOD
   for the rest of my life.
Death Valley is not your final destination. Keep going!!"

I was drained, but very blessed to have been able to share our journey, in the hopes that someone else could receive encouragement. This kind of sharing is an important part of healing.

Through this entire process, Brody's hurt and pain was significant. I really did not fully understand the extent, until he phoned me crying from YC, which is a huge youth convention that takes place every year in Edmonton. Through his tears, he shared that he had been released from the hurt and pain and burden he had carried for so long. My heart soared, and I was so thankful for what God did in his life that weekend. His own Profound Sadness was gone, along with the depression that he had felt. He shared that our time here is short, and it's a waste to focus on anything but being positive and sharing Christ's love with others.

Mike was, and is, very private with his pain. Most times, out of my own pain, I interpreted his responses as a lack of caring, but this was very far from the truth. It had caused some big fights over these years, as my accusations of him to what I perceived as his heartless responses would provoke a reaction that, although was justified, made it feel like we were being torn apart. But God knows what He is doing, and the wisdom he had in bringing Mike and me together. It took me a LONG time to get to the place where I could love and release and not concern myself over Kaci's day-to-day events. Mike had simply learned that lesson long before me.

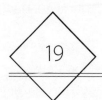

19

THE END IS NOT THE END

I put off writing this book for a long time. I would write, and then stop, going at times eight months or more without writing. I felt like there should be some crazy, radical, miracle sort of ending to wrap this all up in a neat little package with some kind of resolution, so that now you the reader can have closure and know that everything is again right with the world. Well, that is not the case, and not really the point.

Yes, this journey has taken me "Over the Falls". So much of the time, I never knew what the day would bring; I still don't. I spend each morning praying for protection for Kaci and asking God to preserve her life. I still get calls that she is having a meltdown. Hormones and addiction are an ugly two-headed beast.

Yes, these years have been the darkest I have faced, darker than I could have imagined. But "ending well" isn't really the point. The point is that we will all go through hard times with people. It could be a parent or sibling, friend or child. I used to have a Harley frame in my living room that said, "It's not the destination; it's the journey." We are all on a journey. Everyone's journey is different. We are all supposed to learn something different on our journey. We can choose to let the journey change and grow us, or we can blame the journey and become bitter and critical and miserable. We can be the victim, or the victor. We can embrace defeat, or celebrate being an overcomer. We can declare victory over our darkness even when it's dark, or we can buckle under the weight of despair.

I responded to my situation in the way I truly feel God asked. I fell short many times, as I have shared in these pages, but I have learned, am learning, to listen and respond. It has been brutally tough, and I have wanted to throw in the towel multiple times. I am no spiritual super hero. Even a month ago I was like: "God, are you even there? Do you even care, or have you forgotten about us?" And literally the next day, in church, a lady named Susan came up to Mike and me during the singing and asked to pray for us. A bit unusual, maybe, but as she prayed, God spoke through her directly to us and said, "You are doing what I have asked you to do. Even in the little things that nobody sees, you have been obedient. I am pleased. Stay on the path I have for you. My blessings are abundant." The timing and the message were what I needed, when I needed it.

I have often felt like I stood at the door to clinical depression, and all I had to do was open the door and fall. If I chose to walk through the door, it would be a place I may never be able to leave. I had to choose to go for a walk instead, or reach out to a friend. I had to resolve to myself that I wanted better for my life.

The last three years have been quite a journey. Where are things at now? I am so glad you asked! We have Sundays dinners every week, and Kaci and her boyfriend attend. I talk to her every day and see her several times a week. We have made peace with the past, and I can see how God is working in her life. She is coming into a new understanding of God and life and family, and is making positive changes. To be clear, there is no real resolution per se. I have let go of the idea that she will ever live with me again. She is on her own journey. I pray for her daily and believe that whatever God chooses to allow into her life is a part of His plan for her.

As I wrap up this book, my friend Adeline is battling cancer. I hope I get the chance to share this book with her. Her attitude and response to her illness is truly remarkable and I want to share it with you: She does not question her faith. In response to her latest stage 4 diagnosis, she said to her eldest daughter, "Do we only accept good gifts from God? No. We accept all things that come to us, as lessons, as faith builders, as relationship growers and love binders. I know that prayers for healing have not yet been answered, but that's because it's not a vending machine. God has answered so many other prayers, and I trust and there are many 'party-worthy' surprises to come! I don't plan to change a thing. I'll live every new adventurous day to the fullest, collecting each precious moment in his hourglass sands of time."

She goes onto write:

I am devastated… but not deserted

… I am crushed…but not cynical

… I am heartbroken … but not hopeless

… I am distressed… but not destroyed

…I am fearful…but not frantic

... I am perplexed... but not without purpose

"We carry this treasure (faith) around in the frail, unadorned clay pots of our lives... so that the power might be from God... not from us" 2 Corinthians 4: 7-12

Wow. Imagine yourself in her shoes. I don't know about you, but to me, her response to what seems a hopeless situation is beautiful. I pray that as you weather the storms in your own life you will:

1. RELEASE your situation to God.

2. Choose to surrender your FEAR to him.

3. SEEK and ASK what you need to do or not do.

4. Rise above your feelings and circumstance and CHOOSE your response.

5. TRUST that His plans for you are good, and that nothing is impossible with God.